T0283910

The Women
Who Built Omaha

A Bold and Remarkable History

EILEEN WIRTH

University of Nebraska Press
Lincoln

The University of Nebraska Press is part of a land-grant institution
with campuses and programs on the past, present, and future
homelands of the Pawnee, Ponca, Otoe-Missouria, Omaha, Dakota,
Lakota, Kaw, Cheyenne, and Arapaho Peoples, as well as those of the
relocated Ho-Chunk, Sac and Fox, and Iowa Peoples.

Publication of this volume was assisted by a grant from the Friends of
the University of Nebraska Press.

Library of Congress Cataloging-in-Publication Data
Names: Wirth, Eileen M., 1947– author.
Title: The women who built Omaha : a bold and remarkable history /
Eileen Wirth.
Description: Lincoln : University of Nebraska Press, [2022] | Includes
bibliographical references and index.
Identifiers: LCCN 2021037033
ISBN 9781496228642 (paperback)
ISBN 9781496231246 (epub)
ISBN 9781496231253 (pdf)
Subjects: LCSH: Women—Nebraska—Omaha—Biography. | Women—
Nebraska—Omaha—Social conditions. | Omaha (Neb.)—History. |
Omaha (Neb.)—Social conditions. | BISAC: HISTORY / United States /
State & Local / Midwest (IA, IL, IN, KS, MI, MN, MO, ND, NE, OH, SD,
WI) | HISTORY / Women
Classification: LCC F674.O553 A285 2022 | DDC 305.409782/254—dc23
LC record available at https://lccn.loc.gov/2021037033

Set in Bulmer MT by Mikala R. Kolander.

To my daughter, Shanti Psota,
and to my Creighton alums, who I hope will be
inspired by the women of this book

Contents

Illustrations

Preface

In the late 1930s Omaha, Nebraska, was a grimy, blue-collar city with railroad shops and lead smelters on the Missouri River, the enormous stockyards in South Omaha, a warehouse district downtown, and bars everywhere. The Federal Writers' Project described it as "distinctly a man's town."[1] But about this time a wealthy, utterly determined young woman launched a lifelong crusade to beautify Omaha, especially its parks, changing the face of her city.

Rachel Gallagher and the parks became virtually synonymous. By the time she died in 1977, she had blocked Interstate 80 from touching Riverview Park, preserving it to become today's Henry Doorly Zoo and Aquarium and prevented the University of Nebraska at Omaha from expanding into midtown's beloved Elmwood Park. She led the parks board and played a major role in the city charter's adoption, opening doors to women in city government. Yet Gallagher is one of many women whose roles in shaping Omaha's history have been overlooked in histories of Omaha. This book seeks to fill that gap.

This is a book about the women who built Omaha, Nebraska, but whose contributions have been forgotten or downplayed. It covers the activities of noteworthy local women in numerous fields and from varied racial and ethnic backgrounds from the

1850s, when Omaha was founded along the banks of the Missouri River, to the modern women's movement in the 1970s, with a nod to the present day.

While Omaha's men were building railroads and banks, its women were building schools and hospitals. They were endowing universities, building art museums, fighting for the right to vote, and running houses of ill repute and bootlegging. Yet women and women's groups constitute only about 10 percent of the names in the indexes of two major local histories written a century apart. A reader would never know that women founded or transformed Creighton University, Joslyn Art Museum, Mutual of Omaha, the Henry Doorly Zoo, and so much more.

Is Omaha a "man's town," as the Federal Writers' Project asserted, or is it a male-centered town where women have not gotten credit for all they have contributed? This book will demonstrate that the latter is true. The city has a much richer women's history than has been previously recognized.

To give a sense of chronology in a book that focuses on what women have accomplished in various fields, the book begins with a description of Omaha and its women during the 1850s–70s. Three "interlude chapters" throughout the book describe Omaha in various eras and discuss how local and national events and trends impacted local women. These chapters also provide some historical context for events that span the book.

Most chapters outline the history of women in particular fields and tell their stories. The earlier chapters focus on institutions, fields, and movements in which women were involved during the nineteenth century. Later chapters focus on fields like law and local government in which women's presence was rare until modern times. Two chapters focus on the discriminatory way Omaha has treated its African American and Indian residents and the contributions women from these groups have made.

The book ends with an overview of the changes the women's

movement in the 1970s brought to Omaha's women and their city. Although there is no chapter on women in the media specifically— because my previous book *From Society Page to Front Page* covers local women journalists—stories by women journalists were a rich source of information on what women have done for Omaha.

More women made significant contributions to every field than the book could cover. It features women and groups of women who were groundbreakers in opening their fields to women; started major businesses or institutions or rose to power in male-dominated businesses and institutions; battled racial and gender discrimination; were leaders in important events in the city of Omaha such as the Trans-Mississippi and International Exposition; and/or exemplified the contributions of many women to fields such as family businesses and education.

The book profiles women from many backgrounds, but upper-class women are overrepresented because they have traditionally been allowed greater access to civic life and their histories were more likely to have been recorded. This overrepresentation also reflects the clout that money confers in Omaha. Rich women could decide how to spend their money, even when most women had few legal rights. Mea culpa to the many worthy women—and women's organizations—who have been omitted.

This book is based on original research, including numerous interviews with descendants of the profiled women and, when possible, the women themselves. Experts in various fields recommended women they believed should be profiled. Omaha Public Library local history librarians Martha Grenzeback and Lynn Sullivan suggested many names and sources of information.

The bibliography includes all print and online sources as well as a list of individuals I interviewed. Much of the best material came from *Omaha World-Herald* articles accessed online.

As an early baby boomer, I helped break gender barriers in local journalism. This personal history influenced my selection of the stories of women who left their mark on a male-dominated city. I urge historians to study them in more depth.

Meanwhile, I hope readers will realize how many women in various fields have made a major difference in a supposed man's town. Enjoy learning about these extraordinary women.

The Women Who Built Omaha

Introduction

Women in Early Omaha

Early Omaha was a terrible place to live, especially for genteel women settlers from the East. Their accounts describe a primitive village on the Missouri River where they endured everything from hogs in the streets to living in shacks. Nevertheless, early residents believed that Omaha would become a great city. This tendency to envision a great future probably helped them endure their lives. The first women contributed to this vision by establishing schools, building churches, and attending social events that resembled upper-class life in the East. They helped turn Omaha into a bearable home.

When affluent, cultured eastern women came to Omaha on the plains of eastern Nebraska Territory, they settled into a village with unpaved streets that turned extremely muddy during wet weather. Some mud holes were so deep that horses sank belly-deep into them.[1] They suffered through dust storms during dry weather, wandering stray dogs that attacked people, and roaming hogs that fed on garbage in the streets. Omaha smelled bad; human waste from outdoor privies ran into the streets, and some people kept cattle and sheep. The town did not get its first paved street until 1877.

Women had to carry "water from well or cistern except when they could induce their husbands to carry it for them, and the old wood cook stove and later on the base burner were to be found in every home." For its first thirteen years Omaha lacked street-cars, water mains, sewers, and gas or electric lights. For several years not one single home in Omaha had a bathtub.[2] Despite such conditions, settlers, including eastern women unaccustomed to such hardships, still moved to the future city.

Women during Omaha's First Days

Women from Council Bluffs were among the founders of Omaha. They joined men in ferrying across the Missouri River from the Bluffs on July 4, 1854, to hold the picnic that established Omaha. The picnic was illegal because the U.S. Congress had forbidden white settlers to enter Nebraska until it approved a treaty with the Omaha, Otoe, and Missouri tribes that ceded their claims to the territory.[3]

The festivities—which were never intended to last more than that day—ended abruptly when a gunpowder salute not only allegedly frightened the women but attracted some Indians, who appeared on the horizon. Supposedly to avoid endangering the women, the group packed up and hastened to their waiting fer-ryboat to return home.[4]

A week after the picnic, word arrived that the treaties had been approved. A couple named Newell (their first names have been lost to history), who took the morning ferry from Council Bluffs, became Omaha's first residents but only stayed three weeks. While they were there, the husband worked in a new brickyard, and the wife cooked for its employees.

That afternoon William and Rachel Snowden came to Omaha to stay. They managed a crude log boardinghouse/hotel that the Council Bluffs & Nebraska Ferry Company had built for employ-ees at Twelfth and Jackson Streets. It was called the St. Nicholas but was better known as the Claims House.

After living there for three months, the Snowdens built their own log house on Tenth Street on a lot that the ferry company had given them because Mrs. Snowden was the new town's first woman settler. The Snowdens' new home, the town's first private dwelling, used aprons and quilts as windows and doors.[5]

However, Omaha's status as Nebraska's territorial capital made it stand out from other struggling river towns even before its selection as the eastern terminus of Union Pacific Railroad guaranteed its future. The town attracted residents who sensed its potential, and they began improving it.

Creating Omaha Society

Emily Doane, who moved to Omaha in 1859 with her attorney husband, William, discovered how much she would have to tolerate in her new home shortly after her arrival when a gust of wind blew the cape of her dress over her head: "When I pulled it down and looked about me, I saw streets that were mostly a sea of mud, for there were no pavements and only one sidewalk in town, a makeshift affair that surrounded the Herndon House. Here and there a thoughtful citizen had laid a plank or two for the comfort of pedestrians but these were few and far between."[6]

The 1858 opening of the Herndon House hotel at Ninth and Farnam Streets gave Omaha's social life a boost and made life less bleak.[7] Frequent dances and parties to which men wore suits and women elaborate dresses gave Omaha a "certain cosmopolitanism." The gowns had trains for, as Doane said, "no lady would have allowed an ankle to be seen in those days."

Well-bred Omahans attempted to re-create the lives they had formerly known. When parties were held outside Herndon House, the Doanes (who initially lived there) walked to them through the mud, William guiding Emily with a lantern.[8] Most Omaha housing was primitive. Mrs. Experience Estabrook, wife of the territorial attorney general, described living in the equivalent of a barn with a prairie grass roof that leaked badly during heavy rains.[9]

In 1855 the city held an inaugural ball at the City Hotel at Eleventh and Harney Streets, honoring Mark Izard's installation as the first territorial governor. Guests included nine women.[10] Two of the women did not dance, however, so men took their places in square dancing.[11]

First Churches, Schools, and Stores

It took a year or so, but women helped Omaha acquire urban amenities like churches, schools, and stores. Although the city was not very religious, several early congregations held services at the original territorial capitol—Methodists in the morning, Congregationalists in the afternoon, and Baptists at night.[12]

In 1866 Margaret Cuming, the Catholic wife of territorial governor Thomas Cuming, an Episcopalian, persuaded her husband to donate two lots at Eighth and Howard Streets to build St. Mary's Catholic Church, Omaha's first house of worship.[13]

J. Adelaide Goodwill opened Omaha's first school at the original territorial capitol building in 1855 and taught her forty private school pupils there for a semester. She closed her school because the territorial legislature needed to meet in her schoolroom.[14]

Stores began to open. Tootle & Jackson, the first dry goods store, was established in late 1854 and was followed by a drugstore in 1855. Meanwhile, the Council Bluffs & Nebraska Ferry Company was selling lots and promoted settlement.[15]

Omaha's first theatrical performance was held in the dining room of the Herndon House in 1860 and featured Julia Dean Hayne, an eminent actress of the period.[16] In 1867 the first real theater, the Academy of Music, opened on the Caldwell Block at Thirteenth and Douglas Streets. It attracted famous performers in plays, operas, and concerts.[17]

Growth of the City

Within a dozen years Omaha had grown rapidly westward since it could not expand farther east. An 1866 city map shows Omaha's boundaries as roughly Seward Street on the north, Linn Street (today's Castelar Street) on the south, and Thirtieth Street on the west, although most development ended at Twenty-Fourth Street. The ferry landed on the site of today's CHI Center. Central High School occupies the site of the second territorial capitol building.

The commercial district was centered around today's Gene Leahy Mall, while the first residential district stretched from the river to Twenty-Second and Burt Streets, with only one home west of today's Central High School. Early businesses included a newspaper, a bakery, a pharmacy, a liquor distributor, and dry goods stores. Eventually, the business district absorbed parts of the initial residential area as home builders moved west, north, and southeast. The most desirable neighborhoods were the capitol (Central High) area and along South Tenth Street.[18]

City on a Bluff

Union Pacific Railroad put Omaha on the national map. After the Civil War, railroad construction started in Omaha and moved west to Utah, where it drove the golden spike to link up with the Central Pacific in 1869. The nation had its first transcontinental railroad, and Omaha was transformed into a small city with great ambitions. One of the city's visitors in 1867, while construction was in progress, was *New York Herald* reporter Henry Stanley, who described Omaha as "beautifully located on a high-level plateau" above the Missouri River. He noted that "on one of these hills is the territorial capitol surrounded by a park 600 feet square . . . Below the city with its wide regular streets, business blocks, churches and buildings. There the railroad winding

5

from huge machine shops around the city, then cutting through the hills passes on its way mills, warehouses and gardens."[19]

Although Omaha still had no paved streets when Stanley visited, it was no longer a mud village clinging precariously to the riverbank.

1

Education

Teaching was the only career open to educated women for decades. Consequently, education in Omaha has always been primarily a women's field, often run by men. Women have taught the students in the city's public, Catholic, and other private schools while facing gender and racial discrimination. This chapter examines the role of women in building the Omaha Public Schools (OPS), Omaha's Catholic schools, and Brownell Hall, an elite private school for girls that held Omaha's first high school graduation.

Omaha Public Schools

Women in Early Omaha Public Schools

By 1859 Omaha operated three one-room public schools that closed during the Civil War due to lack of funding but reopened after the war. Ten years later the Nebraska Legislature donated the old territorial capitol building to Omaha for use as a high school, but it was torn down in 1870 because it was deemed unsafe. The following year the new $225,000 building housing Omaha High School (OHS) opened on the site at Twentieth and Dodge.[1] The imposing structures housed both elementary and high school classes and featured a landmark clock tower. Initial high school enrollment was only forty-seven students, rising to sixty a year later.[2]

In 1876 nine of the eleven members of the first graduating class were girls; they posed for an all-female graduation portrait in fancy white dresses rather than caps and gowns.[3] Two years later the four-member graduating class was all-female, although later classes reflected a more even gender balance.[4] Nationally, girls dominated early high schools because boys did not need a high school degree to get a good job, while girls who finished high school could teach in elementary schools.[5] Dr. Keith Bigsby, former principal of Central High, said he believes that this was the case at Omaha High School.[6] By 1894 OHS had grown to about a thousand students.[7]

Women dominated elementary schools, but a majority of early OHS teachers were men, especially in math and science, though foreign language teachers were mostly women, according to Bigsby. Women were paid less and were expected to leave teaching when they married. A morals clause in contracts encouraged church attendance, but OHS teachers were not required to teach Sunday school, as they were in some small towns in Nebraska.[8]

Central's curriculum included several tracks, but most emphasized English, foreign languages, political and social sciences, mathematics, and the sciences.[9] In 1885 the school introduced manual training for both genders, with the girls' program focused on domestic science.[10]

Omaha High School, which began to be called Central High between 1911 and 1913, offered girls numerous cocurricular opportunities such as joining Cadet Battalion Company Z, which taught girls "to drill like the boys."[11] In 1903 students formed the Margaret Fuller Society in honor of the nineteenth-century author, feminist, and champion of women's education. Two years later the school formed the Frances Willard Society, in honor of this suffragist, educator, and temperance reformer.[12] By 1906 the student newspaper, the *Register*, had its first woman editor.[13] Early yearbooks show girls involved in numerous athletic activities, clubs, and academic organizations. The building included separate gyms for boys and girls.

Central High's First Female Principal

When Kate McHugh was named the first woman principal of Omaha High in 1911, it was major news, as was her forced retirement in 1914.[14] The newspaper article announcing her retirement said it was required by a state law that applied only to Omaha's public schools and called her one of the nation's most outstanding educators.[15]

McHugh had become principal when today's building was being constructed; new sections formed a square around an open space in the middle where the old building had stood. Officials disagreed about what to do with the open space.

Bigsby said he believes that McHugh was forced out because she favored using the open space as a courtyard, while some board members wanted to rebuild the old building's clock tower there.[16] However, newspaper stories about McHugh's tenure as principal say nothing about such a dispute, and no one at Central today knows about the state law the newspaper article referenced.

There's no question, however, that McHugh was a strong principal who founded Central's student council, hired its first debate coach, and turned debate into a class.[17] She also had a powerful impact on students. "Some of us oldsters remember the charming personality and dedicated teaching of Miss Kate McHugh. She was a profound scholar, an authority on Shakespeare and the first woman principal of a high school in Omaha. Miss McHugh did more for Omaha . . . than others who have their names used in the dedication of new schools."[18] The "Public Pulse" letter was written by a former student, Ralph Sweeley. A newspaper note explained who McHugh was.

McHugh, a native of Galena, Illinois, began teaching second grade there when she was only eighteen. She taught high school

English there, too, and served as high school principal before joining Omaha High School as an English teacher in 1893.[19] She chaired the English Department before becoming OHS assistant principal and then principal. The 1914 yearbook called her "the most popular teacher, having a charm of manner and gift of expression."[20]

As principal, she tolerated no nonsense. In 1914 she expelled seven members of a group that called itself the "High School Bums" for wearing old-fashioned dress suits and cowboy outfits to school.[21] She also asked boys not to smoke within two blocks of the school.[22] Some students recalled McHugh's kindness. For example, C. A. Franklin, an Omaha native who published the *Kansas City Call*, a major African American newspaper, called himself her protégé and always visited her when he returned to Omaha.[23]

After retiring from Central, McHugh joined Omaha University's English Department, and the university awarded her an honorary degree in 1919.[24] She also was the first woman president of the Nebraska State Teachers' Association, an organizer of the Omaha Drama League in 1915, and a member of the Omaha Library Board. McHugh died in Santa Barbara, California, in 1931. After her death Central faculty members donated a portrait of her that has since been lost.[25] Faculty members also donated to a scholarship in her memory.[26] In 2021 OPS promoted Ellisa Kirksey from assistant principal to principal, making her the school's second woman principal.

The District Acquires Benson High and Principal Mary McNamara

The Omaha Public Schools gained a second woman high school principal, Mary McNamara, when Omaha annexed the town of Benson in 1917. McNamara served as principal of Benson High School from 1911 to 1950, said retired Benson dean of students Joan Fogarty.[27] McNamara was noted for having "an idea of the right way to do things and you did it her way." "She was strict with her faculty and personnel. She taught the faculty the concepts of excellent classroom instruction," according to Fogarty. "She was in classrooms all the time and never missed a major school event. Her job was her life." Benson High has kept McNamara's legacy alive with scholarships and awards named in her honor. Students considered it a distinction to attend Benson, and many of them became top civic leaders.[28] McNamara died in 1969.

With exceptions like McHugh and McNamara, the principals of OPS high schools were men until the modern women's movement. However, women were frequently elementary school principals. Until the late 1960s, African Americans of both genders struggled just to be hired, although Lucinda "Lucy" Gamble Williams broke the race barrier in 1895.

Lucinda Gamble Williams: The District's First African American Teacher

Lucy Gamble, one of the first two African Americans to graduate from Omaha High School, became OPS's first African American teacher in 1895. Gamble, who was born in Lincoln, moved to Omaha with her family in 1880. After high school she graduated from the Omaha Normal School, which trained teachers. For six years she taught at Dodge School and then Cass School, the latter predominately white. When she quit teaching to marry the Reverend John Williams, pastor of St. Philip's Episcopal Church, the *Omaha World-Herald* devoted a full column to the wedding (this was unusual because the paper did not routinely carry African American weddings until the 1970s).

Williams, whose husband died in 1933, returned to teaching adult education for OPS at the Urban League Community Center during the 1930s, and she also taught classes at the North Side YWCA, in addition to being active in church and community volunteer work. She served numerous groups, including the North Side YWCA, the Colored Old Folks Home, and the Omaha Community Chest, leading citywide arts committees. Williams and her husband raised three children. She died in Omaha in 1956.[29]

The Groundbreaking Work of Katherine Fletcher

Katherine Fletcher, the first African American teacher at North Omaha's Kellom Elementary School, also served as its principal. In 1974 she broke another barrier when she was named principal of Laura Dodge School, making her the first Black principal of a West Omaha school.[30]

Fletcher, a West Virginia native, moved to Omaha after World War II to marry her husband, Omahan Wanasabee Fletcher, a jazz musician and teacher whom she met while he was stationed in Washington DC during the war. She joined OPS in 1948 and spent forty years with the district. Her accomplishments included starting Nebraska's first school breakfast program and directing the OPS Child and Youth Study Program. She was noted for working to bridge the differences between racial groups. In 2014 Girls Incorporated named its North Omaha Center in her honor.[31] Fletcher was one of many outstanding women elementary school principals in Omaha Public Schools, but she worked for a school system that was blatantly racist into the 1960s.

Dr. Cheryl Logan Leads the Modern School District

When Dr. Harry Burke was OPS superintendent, from 1946 to 1962, he hired Black teachers for only two segregated elementary schools and refused to hire Black teachers for high school. He was also known for demeaning Black teachers.[32]

Today Dr. Cheryl Logan, OPS's first female and first African American superintendent, heads a district that Burke would not recognize. According to OPS statistics, more than 70 percent of its students are children of color, and only 28 percent are white.[33] In addition, four of nine OPS board members are African American, including its 2020 president, Marque Snow.[34] Much of this change reflects the movement of whites to the Millard and Elkhorn Public Schools in West Omaha. When the City of Omaha annexed those towns, their school districts remained independent.

Logan's OPS is distinctly urban, and she was chosen because of her success in urban districts. Elsewhere she had previously been chief academic officer of the School District of Philadelphia and had been an elementary and high school principal in Prince George's Public Schools in Maryland.[35]

Controversy over Burke's racist legacy was heightened in 2020, the summer of George Floyd's killing by police in Minneapolis and global protests by the Black Lives Matter movement. At the peak of the protests, an *Omaha World-Herald* editorial urged that Burke High School be renamed for Lucy Gamble. The editorial noted that Logan opposes naming schools for people, so the name remained unchanged.[36]

Omaha Catholic Schools

Omaha's Catholic schools, which enroll about twenty thousand children in the twenty-three-county archdiocese, began in the 1860s as part of a national church effort to educate children in their faith and preserve their ethnic heritage. Protestants dominated the public schools at that time. Thousands of Catholic nuns taught for almost nothing, making the new schools financially possible.[37]

Bishop James O'Gorman, who had made education his top priority, won a major victory when he persuaded the Sisters of Mercy to come teach in Omaha. The Irish order, whose mission was to serve the "poor, the sick, and the ignorant," came to the United States during the potato famine, when many Irish emigrated because they went where the need was greatest, according to Sister Susan Severin, RSM, an archivist for the order.[38] During the Civil War, while many Sisters of Mercy nursed both Union and Confederate soldiers, seven of them headed west to the poor diocese of Omaha on a harrowing journey through guerrilla-infested territory.[39]

Mercy Sisters Pioneer Local Catholic Schools

To reach Omaha, the sisters had traveled from Chicago through Illinois and Missouri. In St. Joseph, Missouri, they spent the night in a hotel that resembled a barn, then boarded a steamer to Omaha.[40] When they stepped off the ferry in 1864, curious onlookers, including some Native Americans, stared at their black habits, elaborate coifs, and veils. The sisters were reportedly shocked by their new home.[41]

O'Gorman met them at the ferry and walked them up muddy hills to St. Mary's Convent at today's Twenty-Fourth Street and St. Mary's Avenue. The unfurnished three-story brick building included classrooms on the second floor and living quarters on the third.[42] The sisters slept on the floor that first night, then walked to St. Mary's Church downtown for morning Mass. Afterward they borrowed tin cups for their breakfast coffee.[43]

It was an inauspicious beginning for Omaha's Catholic school system, but the sisters were adventurers. "They had to be adventurous because when they came to the U.S., they knew they would never return to Ireland and would never see their families again," said Severin.[44]

A local paper, the *Nebraskan*, called the arrival of the sisters in Omaha "a new era in its history." "The Sisters are accomplished in every branch of science and will attract scores of young ladies from every portion of the West. . . . It is for the interest of Omaha and every businessman in it to build up the school. No one thing adds more to the importance of a place than good educational advantages."[45]

Every morning the sisters walked the two miles to their school no matter the weather, starting fires to heat freezing classrooms in the winter. In November 1864 they opened Mount Saint Mary's

Academy in their convent, where they also housed orphans. The academy hoped to attract regional students who might otherwise have gone to school in the East.

Promotional materials stressed the school's beauty and culture but failed to mention that during blizzards the sisters, pupils, and orphans huddled around stoves that could not keep the convent warm.[46] Eventually, the sisters sold their outdated convent and moved to other locations as the number of schools they established continued to grow. They founded nineteen grade schools and two high schools that merged into today's Mercy High School. In 1923 they founded the College of Saint Mary to prepare women to teach in church schools.

The small orphanage in the convent grew into the large St. James Orphanage (since closed) in the Benson area, and the order also opened St. Joseph Hospital, which became Creighton University's teaching hospital, before selling it to Franciscans because the Sisters of Mercy were spread too thin.[47] Later they opened St. Catherine's Hospital, predecessor of today's CHI Health Creighton University Medical Center–Bergan Mercy. Their regional headquarters for the western United States is still in Omaha.

Other religious orders joined the Sisters of Mercy in staffing Omaha's numerous Catholic grade and high schools. These included the Servants of Mary (Marian High School), the Religious of the Sacred Heart (Duchesne Academy), the Sisters of Notre Dame (Notre Dame Academy, which has closed), and the School Sisters of St. Francis (Ryan High School, which has also closed). The various orders also staffed numerous parish elementary schools. Marian, Mercy, and Duchesne remain all-girl high schools.

Lay Women in Catholic Schools

Changes in religious life after the Vatican II Council in the 1970s led to a sharp decline in the number of nuns, threatening Catholic education. However, lay teachers and administrators, mostly women, took their places and kept Catholic schools alive. The shift in staffing was dramatic.

In 1948, 98 percent of the teachers in Omaha's Catholic elementary schools were religious women, while only 2 percent were laypeople. Fifty years later the ratio was reversed, and most of today's Catholic elementary schools are staffed entirely by lay teachers and administrators, still heavily female.[48]

Outstanding lay principals have included Bonnie Pryor of St. Cecilia's Grade School, who opened a day care center for faculty and parents in her school and offered one of Omaha's first after-school care programs. The National Catholic Educational Association named her one of the nation's top fifty Catholic educators. Numerous lay-run Catholic schools have won National Blue Ribbon awards for excellence from the U.S. Department of Education, including all-female Marian High School in 2020.

Non-Catholic Private Schools

Today's Omaha includes a variety of non-Catholic private schools run by other religious denominations, but one outstanding private school, today's Brownell-Talbot, is also one of the oldest and originally was all-female.

Brownell Hall

In 1868 all-female Brownell Hall held Nebraska's first high school graduation. Episcopalians had founded the boarding school for elite girls to allow them to be educated in the region instead of the East.[49]

Brownell Hall, which opened three miles north of Omaha in 1863, is named for the Connecticut Episcopal bishop who funded it. Originally, students were confined to the school's grounds because of fears about Native Americans who lived in the area. Girls rose at 6:00 a.m. for a day of classes, religious services, study, and recreation, including playing croquet, before lights out at 9:00 p.m.[50] Brownell's college preparatory curriculum included languages, science, literature, and composition in addition to physical culture and domestic science classes. On Fridays girls read their compositions aloud, recited poems, and did their mending.[51]

Nebraska Episcopal bishop Robert Clarkson opened the school to day students in 1868, and he and his wife, Meliora, moved to its second location at Sixteenth and Jones Streets. Mrs. Clarkson served as matron and housekeeper.[52] By 1891 Brownell reached a "high water of attendance," with seventy-three boarders and fifty-two day students.[53] Virtually all teachers were women.

Brownell moved to its current location in Dundee in 1922.[54] Thirty years later it started a Brownell Hall–Talbot School for Boys, before being renamed Brownell Talbot School in 1963. Four years later it became independent of the Episcopal Church, and it remains a prestigious coed school for students from preschool through high school.[55]

The school's distinctions include educating most of the state's early women artists. When it began researching the state's early women artists for an exhibit, the Museum of Nebraska Art (MONA) in Kearney discovered Brownell's important role in producing women artists, according to retired MONA director Audrey Kauders.[56] Early alums also include Harriet Dakin McMurphy, Nebraska's first woman journalist, who crusaded for food safety legislation during her long *Omaha World-Herald* career. She would have been in Brownell's first graduating class if she had not been behind on her Latin requirement.[57]

Closing Notes

Local histories pay little attention to the development of education in Omaha and largely ignore the women who taught in all types of schools. The Sisters of Mercy, for example, are almost entirely overlooked despite their work not only in education but in health and human services. When they are recognized, it is usually for their hospitals.

Similarly, even Central High promoters seem to know little about Kate McHugh, and OPS's African American groundbreaker, Lucy Gamble Williams, is largely unknown. Teaching remains one of the most underpaid professions, possibly because such a high percentage of teachers have always been women. On a more positive note, more women hold top administrative posts in all types of schools, and both OPS and the Catholic schools present major awards to outstanding teachers.

2

Founding Creighton University and Duchesne

In 1875 Omaha's richest widow, Mary Lucretia Creighton, was
the sole heir to the fortune that her late husband, Edward, had
earned by building the transcontinental telegraph, founding First
National Bank, cattle ranching, and other enterprises. When she
signed her will bequeathing $100,000 to start a Catholic college
for boys, she gave Omaha its first university.

So where did the idea of starting a university come from?
Edward, who had no will, had died suddenly in 1874, two days
after collapsing at his desk from a possible stroke. He was only
fifty-four. Since he had left no instructions on how to use his
money, Mary Lucretia made those decisions.[1] Creighton University
versity lore suggests that Edward had told his wife he wanted to
start a college, but no one knows for sure, according to Creighton
ton University historian Dennis Mihelich. At any rate, Edward
did nothing to set this plan in motion, although other wealthy
telegraph business associates, such as the Cornell family, owners
of Western Union, were founding colleges bearing their names.[2]

Both Mary Lucretia and her sister Sarah Emily (wife of
Edward's brother and business partner, John) were interested
in education because their husbands were not well educated,
said Ann McGill, one of their descendants. "When the brothers
had business dealings with people in the East, they were acutely

aware of their lack of education. This was a motivator for starting a university."[3]

Mary Lucretia died six months after making her will, leaving John, Sarah Emily, and Bishop James O'Connor to start a Catholic college in a community of fewer than thirty thousand people. In creating Creighton, they helped transform "Omaha from a post–Civil War river town to a prosperous late nineteenth century city," wrote the Reverend John Schlegel, sj, Creighton president from 2000 to 2011.[4]

Mary Lucretia and Sarah Emily Wareham Creighton

Mary Lucretia and Sarah Emily Creighton were the daughters of David Wareham of Dayton, Ohio, a builder and political leader who became friends with Edward Creighton when he was building telegraph lines out of Dayton. Edward moved to Omaha in 1856 but returned to Dayton to marry Mary Lucretia later that year. They permanently settled in Omaha in 1861. Wareham also moved to Omaha and worked for Edward until he died, in 1864, although his wife remained in Dayton.[5] In Omaha, Edward became general superintendent of the Pacific Telegraph Company.[6]

Mary Lucretia's younger sister Emma (who changed her name to Sarah Emily) met Edward's younger brother John while visiting her sister in Omaha. After she and John married, in 1868, they lived with the Creightons for years.[7] Both couples were left childless after the deaths of infant children, but other Creighton siblings joined them in Omaha and had numerous descendants, some of whom still live in the city.[8]

All four Creightons were devout Catholics and dedicated philanthropists, but family lore suggests the sisters had very different personalities. "Mary Lucretia was the pretty one," said descendant Mary Maxwell. "She had lovely eyes. Everyone loved her. Sarah Emily was very stern. She was more of an organizer. She was a hands-on leader and a power in her own right." Far more descendants are named Mary or Lucretia than Sarah or Emily.[9]

Although Mary Lucretia could have built a mansion and lived luxuriously like other rich Omaha women, she spent her days driving her carriage around Omaha's poor neighborhoods, responding to requests for help. Edward gave her twenty-five dollars a day to distribute to the needy.[10] Sarah Emily was equally generous but made large gifts to institutions such as Creighton University and religious orders.

Starting Creighton University

Creighton's founders faced formidable obstacles, despite having a bequest worth about $2.3 million today. Only about a third of the Catholic colleges founded before 1900 survived their first decades. Like the Creightons, most Catholics were either immigrants or first-generation Americans, and few Catholic students were prepared for high school, let alone college. Catholic colleges, including Creighton, normally served younger students and developed them into collegians. In addition, Catholics and their institutions faced hostility in a predominately Protestant nation.[11]

The first hurdle was finding a religious order to run the college. The Creightons had strong ties to the Dominicans, but the Dominicans declined their invitation to run the new school.[12] Bishop O'Connor then invited the Jesuits to do so. After regional Jesuit officials rejected the request over concerns about the location and staffing, O'Connor successfully appealed to Jesuit officials in Rome for approval.[13] This brought Catholicism's most powerful religious community to Omaha.

In 1877 O'Connor used funds from Mary Lucretia's bequest to purchase a seven-acre campus on a hilltop northwest of Capitol Hill. Construction of the original building began in May, and Creighton's first president, the Reverend Roman A. Shaffel, sj, arrived in December. He also was chaplain to the Sisters of Mercy and lived in a cottage adjacent to their convent at Eighteenth and Cass Streets before he could move to Creighton in July 1878.

Classes began on September 2, 1878, with 120 students, a number that grew until it peaked at 170 in January. Some of the students were only six years old. There was no tuition due to Mary Lucretia's bequest, and some students were Protestants. The *Omaha Daily Herald* was the only local newspaper that even reported the event.[14] The first college class did not graduate until 1891.[15]

John and Sarah Emily Help Shape Creighton

John and Sarah Emily helped turn Creighton into a science-oriented college from its first days, an identity that continues today. They helped finance both a Chemical Building and an Observatory during the 1880s, initiating Creighton's enduring emphasis on science education. The Observatory still stands in the Jesuit Gardens adjacent to Creighton Hall, although it is no longer used. After Sarah Emily's death, John, an extremely successful businessman in his own right, continued to underwrite Creighton's operations and also founded its medical school and hospital.[16]

Sarah Emily was especially interested in Creighton's religious identity. She helped persuade the Jesuits to build St. John's Church. The iconic gray sandstone English Gothic church in the heart of today's campus was completed in 1888, although the towers were added later. John donated $10,000 of the $50,000 cost.[17]

Sarah Emily donated two ornate marble side altars, each costing $2,500. One is dedicated to the Blessed Virgin, the other to Saint Joseph. She also donated one of the stained glass windows, the sanctuary carpet, upholstered chairs, and other furnishings. Sarah Emily's sister, Mary Schenk, contributed a $2,500 organ. Other relatives paid for other stained glass windows and the main altar. After Sarah Emily died, in 1888, John donated the church's carved stone Stations of the Cross in her memory.[18]

Sarah Emily also spearheaded the construction of a new south wing on the main college building to house Creighton's growing Jesuit community. It opened in 1889.

Sarah Emily's Other Donations and Funeral

In addition to her joint gifts to Creighton with her husband, Sarah Emily made personal donations to the university, St. Joseph Hospital, St. John's Church, the Poor Clares (a Franciscan order), and other charities from a bequest she had received from Mary Lucretia. Like her sister, she suffered from fragile health and died of a pulmonary disease on September 30, 1888. After her funeral at St. John's Church, she was buried in a family circle at Holy Sepulchre Cemetery around the obelisk that Mary Lucretia had purchased.[19] Her bequests included $50,000 to the Franciscan Sisters of Nebraska to build the new St. Joseph Hospital, which became Creighton's teaching hospital.[20]

Founding Duchesne Academy

After planning for Creighton began, Bishop O'Connor invited the Religious of the Sacred Heart (RSCJ), a prestigious order of French nuns, to come to Omaha to start a school for girls since Creighton was all-male. They rejected his first request, even though he had served as chaplain of a Sacred Heart convent in Pennsylvania. O'Connor persisted, most likely aided by the Jesuits' plans to run Creighton, according to Mary Monson, a retired Duchesne Academy history teacher. "We can assume that O'Connor would have mentioned the Jesuit presence in Omaha and that it encouraged the RSCJs to accept," she explained.[21] Most Sacred Heart schools are located in cities that the Jesuits also serve. RSCJ founder Madeleine Sophie Barat was tutored by her Jesuit brother, and both are noted for educational excellence that emphasizes the liberal arts.[22]

O'Connor purchased Park Place at Thirty-Sixth and Burt Streets, a mile from Creighton, for the future school. The site was weed filled, with not a house in sight.[23] The first Sacred Heart sisters moved temporarily into a small frame house at Ninth and Howard Streets that had "dust an inch thick everywhere, windows fitting loosely and much else that made for hard labor and discomfort as well as poverty." There they established the academy, which attracted twenty boarders when it opened in 1881. The next year construction of a large building at Park Place began, and the academy moved into the building in November. The building on Omaha's second highest hill had steam heat, fireplaces, running water, telephone, bathrooms on every floor, and an elevator. Most rooms had gaslights.[24] Within five years there were eighty pupils.[25]

Following the pattern that Saint Philippine Duchesne established when she brought the Sacred Heart order to the United States, Omaha's Sacred Heart community opened a free day school that eventually taught 250 pupils. They supported it with funding from their boarding school. In 1895, when they could no longer afford to operate it, they turned it over to the Sisters of Mercy.[26]

Students at Duchesne Academy were a mixture of boarders and local girls; they wore uniforms and studied religion, English, history, math, languages, and the fine arts. One of the first boarders was William "Buffalo Bill" Cody's daughter. Girls were prepared for college, although it was unusual for even wealthy young women in the 1880s to get a higher education. While some became teachers, nurses, or nuns, most of them married and volunteered for churches, schools, hospitals, and charitable organizations. "At Duchesne, service was front and center. If you were privileged to have been educated there, you had to carry this into the world," said Monson.[27]

Impact of Duchesne on Omaha's Development

Duchesne Academy helped stimulate the growth of its surrounding neighborhood, as did the Omaha diocese's decision to build St. Cecilia's Cathedral two blocks west of the school. The bishop's residence was located across the street from the school, and wealthy people built large homes along Thirty-Eighth Street.

One stormy June day in 1894, a servant at the bishop's house called Duchesne to say, "Sister, do you know that the roof of your convent is over at the Bishop's house?" Inspection showed that the wind had blown the metal roof of the school wing across the street and deposited it in the bishop's yard. Because summer vacation had begun that afternoon, no children were injured.[28]

Duchesne College

In 1925 the Religious of the Sacred Heart order opened Duchesne College and operated it as Creighton's Women's College until 1936, with graduates receiving their degrees from Creighton. The college gained full accreditation in 1939 and was a small but respected all-female liberal arts college until it closed in 1968, a casualty of declining enrollment.[29]

Creighton admitted women to its professional schools from the early days and opened a summer school that admitted women, mostly nuns teaching in Catholic schools, in 1913.[30] Today a majority of its undergraduates are women.

Celebrating the RSCJ's and the Creighton Sisters' Contributions

The last RSCJs retired and left Omaha in 1916, but the lay administrators who staff Duchesne Academy keep the Sacred Heart tradition alive. Duchesne also operates a preschool serving both girls and boys.

At Creighton the top award for promoting the advancement of women at the university is named for Mary Lucretia and Sarah Emily. It is presented annually during Founders Week, when the university celebrates the memory of all four founding Creightons. The university also has retired the seal featuring profiles of just the brothers and now uses one featuring its name. Wareham Building is named in honor of the sisters' family.

3

Native American Women

When white American women were virtual possessions of their fathers and husbands, Omaha Indian women were decision makers in their families and tribe. This chapter explores that heritage, highlighting the career of Susette "Bright Eyes" LaFlesche, who translated for Standing Bear at his trial. It also describes how in 1898 Omaha put Native people on display at the Trans-Mississippi and International Exposition. It ends with a review of some of the contributions of Native American women to modern Omaha.

Defying orders from authorities not to leave the Omaha Indian Reservation, located about ninety miles north of Omaha, Susette "Bright Eyes" LaFlesche mounted one of the fastest horses of her father, Chief Joseph LaFlesche, and dashed twenty-eight miles to the town of Tekamah. There she would take a test to obtain the certificate she needed to become the reservation's first Indian teacher.

Bright Eyes, twenty-one, the chief's eldest daughter, had returned to the reservation in about 1875, after graduating from a fine private school in New Jersey, in order to teach. And she would not be deterred. But first she had to take the test to be certified. In Tekamah she easily passed the test and obtained her certificate. But then reservation authorities demanded another certificate attesting to her moral character. After she threatened to tell the newspapers, they allowed her to teach.[1] She was becoming the leader her father hoped for.

The Visionary Chief LaFlesche

Joseph LaFlesche was the son of a French fur trader and an Indian mother who grew up with his Omaha Indian relatives. He spent his life straddling the worlds of whites and Native Americans. His predecessor, Chief Big Elk, chose Joseph as the best leader to help the tribe survive the coming of the whites. From having traveled extensively throughout the region, Joseph knew that the traditional Indian way of life based on hunting buffalo was doomed. Joseph believed the key to the Omaha people's survival was assimilation, which would require education.[2]

Joseph's decision to work with the whites split the tribe into a "Chief's party," which opposed educating their children, and a "Young Man's party," which favored their education, among other issues. Local federal authorities supported the Chief's party because "it was not [in] the interest of this class of white men that the Indians should become intelligent, self-supporting farmers," according to a book illustrated by Bright Eyes.[3] Joseph's allies in educating Indians included the Presbyterian Church.

Under the federal treaty that forced the Omaha Tribe onto a 302,000-acre reservation north of Omaha, the church received land for a mission school that opened in 1857. It required students to wear white man's clothing and to speak English. Classes included religion, reading, geography, writing, arithmetic, and vocal music. It was here that Bright Eyes and her siblings received their first education.

LaFlesche required his daughters to speak only English at home and refused to allow any of his daughters to be tattooed with a mark that showed their tribal rank.[4] He also encouraged tribal members to build wood frame houses, to farm individual plots, to speak English, and to become Christians.[5]

At a time when white women were virtually the possessions of their husbands and fathers, Omaha Indian women not only managed household affairs but owned the lodges where people lived as well as all their contents. They could reject parental suggestions, marry whomever they wished, and divorced their husbands by placing their goods outside the lodge. Husbands consulted their wives on all decisions affecting families.[6] When the federal government allocated farm plots on the reservation to men but not unmarried women, the Omaha successfully protested the decision.[7]

Building on this heritage, Chief LaFlesche sent his four daughters to a private school in New Jersey after they completed the mission school, to prepare them to become leaders at a time when most whites thought preparing women for careers was a waste of money. He believed that educating them would help the tribe survive. After Bright Eyes completed her schooling in New Jersey, she returned home to teach on the reservation and to care for her three younger sisters, who moved in with her.

From Teacher to Translator

The LaFlesche sisters were well known throughout the state and hosted guests, including senators and congressmen, who came to the reservation to see how the Omaha lived. Bright Eyes even defeated one of the congressmen at backgammon. This confident young woman, who had lived in the white world in addition to the Native world and spoke both Ponca and English, was the perfect translator when the conflict between Indians and whites came to a head in an Omaha courtroom.

The drama began in 1876, after Indians wiped out General George Custer and his army at the Battle of Little Big Horn. This infuriated U.S. Army generals in the West, who retaliated by rounding up and killing the Plains Indians to make the area safer for white settlement. The federal government's takeover of the neighboring Ponca reservation horrified the peaceful Omaha. The government ordered the Ponca to move to a reservation in Oklahoma, but when Chief Standing Bear refused to leave, the government arrested him. In 1877 Standing Bear relented, and the Ponca made a brutal forced march to Oklahoma. Within a year a third of the tribe had died, including the chief's fourteen-year-old son, Bear Shield, a victim of malaria.

Standing Bear had promised his son that he would bury him in Nebraska as tribal tradition required. In January 1879 he and others set out in a blizzard to walk the five hundred miles back to Nebraska to bury Bear Shield. Two months later the group reached Chief LaFlesche's home on the Omaha Reservation. LaFlesche and Bright Eyes were shocked when they saw the Ponca, including children, suffering from hunger, frostbite, and illness. Soldiers marched the starving band to the military stockade at Fort Omaha, just north of the city.

General George Crook, the fort's commander, was sympathetic to the Ponca and tipped off Thomas Tibbles, a local reporter, who met with Standing Bear at Fort Omaha, then wrote stories for the *Omaha Daily Herald*, which he also sent to newspapers in the East, about the Indian father who merely wanted to bury his son. The public began to rally around Standing Bear, and two of Omaha's top lawyers, Andrew Poppleton and John Webster, volunteered to represent him in federal court. At issue was whether the federal government had the right to imprison Standing Bear and whether he was protected by the United States Constitution. The government maintained that Standing Bear could not sue the federal government because he and other Indians were not citizens, basing this view on the infamous *Dred Scott* case that treated enslaved people as property who had no rights.[8]

Throughout the trial Bright Eyes sat by Standing Bear, translating the proceedings for him as well as translating his moving final plea into English. When Judge Elmer Dundy allowed the chief to address the court, Standing Bear, wearing an eagle feather and a Jefferson medallion, held out his hand to Bright Eyes as she began to translate his stirring words: "That hand is not the color of yours but if I pierce it, I shall feel pain," said the Ponca leader. "If you pierce your hand, you also feel pain. The blood that will flow from mine will be the same color as yours. I am a man. The same God made us both."

Dundy ruled that Indians were people in the eyes of the law and that the federal government had no right to imprison Standing Bear or to force him to return to Oklahoma. He allowed Standing Bear to bury his son in a tribal burial ground near the South Dakota border.[9]

Advocating for Indian Rights

The trial received national attention and generated sympathy for the country's Native American population. To capitalize on this visibility and to raise money to restore the Ponca homeland, the Omaha Ponca Relief Committee organized a lecture tour to Chicago, Boston, and New York featuring Tibbles, Standing Bear, and Bright Eyes.[10] Throughout the three-month tour Bright Eyes impressed the crowds who heard her. She not only translated for Standing Bear but spoke on her own. While Standing Bear dressed in traditional Indian attire, Bright Eyes wore plain dark dresses and eloquently discussed her people, for whom she had almost given up hope. But that was changing, she told an audience in Boston: "I come to you with gladness in my heart and try to thank you for here, after a hundred years of oppression, my people have for the first time found public sympathy and as soon as the truth of their story was known, help was given them."[11]

Bright Eyes disliked it when newspapers patronizingly referred to her as an "Indian princess" or a specimen of an aboriginal race or an "Indian maiden." After all, she spoke five languages, devoured English literature, had published an essay in the *New*

York Times, and wrote poetry.[12] When she met important people such as the poets Henry Wadsworth Longfellow and Oliver Wendell Holmes Sr., she collected their autographs in a journal that her descendants have donated to History Nebraska.[13]

Bright Eyes lectured on Indian rights up and down the East Coast and in foreign countries.[14] Along the way she married Tibbles, a widower who joined her in traveling and advocating for Indian rights.[15] Although they traveled constantly, they maintained their ties to Omaha, the Omaha Tribe, and the LaFlesche family. A Harvard researcher whom they met spent time on the Omaha reservation and raised money to put Susan LaFlesche through medical school.

In 1890 Tibbles, now a *World-Herald* reporter, traveled to South Dakota's Pine Ridge Reservation to cover the clash between the U.S. Army and the Lakota people that is commonly called the Wounded Knee Massacre. Bright Eyes accompanied him. At Wounded Knee the U.S. Cavalry killed more than 250 Lakota men, women, and children in a botched attempt to disarm a camp to which soldiers had escorted the Lakota. When shooting broke out after a Lakota refused to give up his rifle, Bright Eyes helped terrified women and children find shelter away from the battle. Later she tended to the wounded at a church.[16]

Bright Eyes, Native Women, and the Trans-Mississippi Exposition

Bright Eyes also participated in the Trans-Mississippi Exposition of 1898, the world's fair that Omaha hosted to boost the economy after the depression of the 1890s, by illustrating a souvenir book on the Omaha Indians. It was one of several exposition souvenirs and guidebooks, said John Krecek, a retired Creighton administrator who collects fair artifacts.[17]

Omaha acknowledged its Native American roots at the Trans-Mississippi by hosting an Indian Congress representing thirty-five western tribes, but it treated Indians as objects on display for the exposition's 2.6 million visitors, including President William McKinley. The expo's Indian Encampment housed five hundred Indians. "They [Expo leaders] built a grandstand and sold tickets to staged pitched battles between Indians and whites that the Indians always lost," said Krecek. "These were a takeoff on Buffalo Bill's Wild West Show, like modern cowboy and Indian shows. The real West was never like this."[18]

Educational events boasted of government accomplishments in "civilizing" the "aborigines." Visitors observed the lifestyles, culture, and attire of various tribes.[19] Krecek said the exhibits appealed to "the popular imagination of what Indians were like" and emphasized stereotypes of women doing all the work while the men sat around.[20] The Indian Congress showed off women cooking dog meat and living in various forms of housing, including teepees and grass houses.[21] There was no hint of the decision-making roles that women played in their tribes or respectful discussion of various tribal cultures. President McKinley reviewed a parade of Indians in which each tribe was led by women in brilliantly colored blankets. Some had babies strapped on their backs.

Bright Eyes illustrated the small souvenir booklet, *Oo-Mah-Ha Ta-Wa-Tha (Omaha City)*, which carried the text of the treaty between the Omaha and the federal government and profiled major Omaha chiefs, including Joseph LaFlesche. It also contains a few examples of the Omaha people's folklore and tributes to both Omaha and Nebraska in 1898. Many of Bright Eyes's sketches depict Omaha men and women in their Native attire. The book's modern publisher said it was the first book illustrated by a Native American. Today some of Bright Eyes's sketches are in the National Archives.[22] The book's preface by John Webster, who had helped defend Standing Bear, closes with this reflection: "It is hoped that a souvenir of this type will not only recall the wonderful progress made by the white people who have found homes in the valley of the Mississippi, but create and forever perpetuate a kindly feeling for the remnant of the Indian people still remaining and who are slowly struggling upward toward a higher civilization."

The Legacy of Bright Eyes

In 1903 Bright Eyes, who had returned to teaching English on the Omaha Reservation, fell seriously ill. Her sister, Dr. Susan, tended to her, but she died on May 26.[23]

Her family still preserves the heritage of the LaFlesche sisters. Two great-great-nieces, cousins Marguerite Johnson of Lincoln and Carolyn Johnson of Omaha, are descended from Bright Eyes's sister Marguerite. They said that that their mothers always talked more about Dr. Susan than about Bright Eyes because they grew up in Walthill, Nebraska, where Dr. Susan's hospital was located; it is currently being restored.

"When I asked Granny what she remembered about Bright Eyes, she said she was very warm with a warm, funny sense of humor," said Marguerite. "She didn't like being in the limelight. She took on advocacy because of her love of the tribe, but it wasn't her choice."

"She felt a sense of duty and responsibility," added Carolyn. "She was the typical responsible oldest child."

Both Johnsons marveled at the courage that all the LaFlesche sisters showed in leaving their reservation for a boarding school in the East, where they knew no one and had no idea what they would encounter. Family members celebrate their legacy by emphasizing the importance of education and working for social justice through United Methodist Church social ministries.[24]

Contemporary Native American Women

Omaha has between ten thousand and thirteen thousand Native American residents from 164 tribes and nations, although most belong to regional tribes such as the Omaha, Winnebago, Ponca, and Lakota, said Dr. Rudi Mitchell, a former chairman of the Omaha Tribe and a retired Creighton University Native American studies professor. The migration from reservations to cities began in the 1950s, after the federal government passed a Relocation Act to encourage assimilation. It provided transportation and rent until Native Americans found a job.

Mitchell said that most Native Americans who left the reservations initially settled in or just west of downtown Omaha, but they now live all over the city. Most of the men initially worked in packinghouses, while women worked in unskilled manufacturing jobs.

Mothers especially encouraged their children to get educated. For example, Mitchell said that his mother, Mary Mitchell, raised her eight children as a single parent. Five of them got college degrees, including his sister Octa Keen, of Omaha, who taught nursing at the University of Nebraska Medical Center and Clarkson School of Nursing. Mitchell also has three nieces and two great nieces who are doctors.

Another outstanding Native American woman, Tami Buffalohead-McGill, worked in student advising at Creighton University and Nebraska Methodist Health College before retiring. At Creighton she ran a program that mentored Native high school students in Omaha and on reservations applying for Gates Scholarships. These scholarships fully fund college and graduate school for low-income students from minority groups.[25]

The "New Women" of the Gilded Age

Women couldn't yet vote and had to traverse a rapidly growing Omaha in long dresses and layers of petticoats, but at the beginning of the Gilded Age, in the 1880s, a new breed of female activists emerged. They changed not only their own lives but the city.

The Gilded Age, which lasted into the 1890s, was a "turbulent time for women," according to Susanne George Bloomfield, who compiled Elia Peattie's *Omaha World-Herald* columns on women. While traditional women stayed home and submitted to God and their husbands, these "new women" insisted on equal educational and employment opportunities, tried to influence politics, and wanted independence instead of bondage in marriage.[1]

Women were on the move whether or not they joined the city's suffragist movement in fighting for the vote in Nebraska's 1882 referendum. Growing numbers earned an education, entered new careers, and volunteered in the human services as well as at major civic events like the Trans-Mississippi Exposition.

The Gilded Age

When the Gilded Age began, in 1880, Omaha's population was about 30,000, double the number of residents in 1870. Ten years later the city had quadrupled in size, although the official population of 140,492 was probably exaggerated.[2] A booming local economy attracted a diverse influx of newcomers, many of whom had immigrated from numerous countries.[3]

Omaha finally boasted of urban amenities such as running water and sewers, paved streets, street railways, electric lights, and telephones. Cultural institutions, including the Omaha Public Library, Lininger Art Gallery, and the Omaha Drama League, opened.

A few tall buildings gave the downtown a city skyline, and rich entrepreneurs built mansions in the suburban Gold Coast (today's Blackstone area). Women shoppers flocked to the new downtown Brandeis department store, where the top-floor Tea Room allowed them to socialize without a male escort.[4] In the *Omaha World-Herald* Peattie mocked rich women for buying their finery in New York or Chicago when they could get everything they needed in Omaha.[5]

However, when one of the nation's worst financial panics hit in 1893, Omaha suffered severely for several years and lost population. To promote local recovery, business leaders organized the Trans-Mississippi and International Exposition, a world's fair that attracted 2.6 million visitors, including President William McKinley. Prominent women, including Sarah Joslyn, ran the educational, cultural, and entertainment activities. The Trans-Mississippi Exposition introduced Joslyn to volunteering for the arts, an outcome that impacted Omaha long after the pavilions surrounding the faux Venetian lagoon vanished.

New Opportunities for Women

During the Gilded Age colleges had become mostly coed, and young women graduates found opportunities besides teaching. In South Omaha's packinghouses, women joined unions to fight for their rights and joined a strike in 1898.[6] Omaha women had founded hospitals that opened nursing schools.

As more Omaha families and businesses acquired telephones,

they heard mostly female voices saying, "Number please" as the phone operator became a woman's occupation. Rich women founded human service agencies staffed mostly by women to help poor women and children. Women journalists such as Peattie chronicled these activities because advertisers insisted newspapers carry stories that interested females, their primary shoppers.

One of the new careers that opened to women was medicine. In 1883 the Omaha Medical College graduated its first woman, Dr. Georgia Arbuckle Fix, who practiced near North Platte. That year Dr. Amelia Burroughs, a homeopath, who had moved to Omaha from Council Bluffs, Iowa, became the city's first woman doctor. By the end of the decade Omaha had six additional women physicians.[7] However, most Nebraska women still held low-paying jobs such as domestic service, and they earned less when they held the same jobs as men, for example, as teachers. Clerical jobs opened with the invention of the typewriter.[8]

Politically, Omaha's new women fought not only for suffrage but also for temperance and pure food legislation. Harriet Dakin MacMurphy of the *Omaha World-Herald* wrote editorials that helped persuade Congress to pass food safety laws. She also served four governors as a food inspector.[9] Wealthy women joined the Omaha Woman's Club, the local affiliate of the General Federation of Women's Clubs that offered a respectable outlet for social activism. Suffragists lost several major battles before Nebraska finally ratified the Nineteenth Amendment to the U.S. Constitution in 1919.

When the United States entered World War I, women volunteered for the Red Cross, knitted for the troops, observed "meatless Mondays," and in some cases temporarily filled jobs vacated by soldiers. President Woodrow Wilson finally endorsed woman's suffrage because of their contributions to the war effort.[10] Women began moving rapidly toward the modern era.

4

Votes for Omaha Women

The fight for woman's suffrage in Nebraska began in 1855, when Amelia Bloomer addressed the territorial legislature, and finally ended in 1919, after the state ratified the Nineteenth Amendment, which gave women the right to vote.

Omahans played a major role in the struggle, which included debates, marches, and failed campaigns to amend the state constitution. National suffrage leaders visited Nebraska, and two major suffrage conventions were held in Omaha. Some Omaha women, however, helped lead the state fight against suffrage because they feared it would damage traditional family values.

For ninety minutes on July 4, 1855, a famous suffragist from Council Bluffs, Iowa, wearing a plain dark dress instead of the pantaloons named for her, exhorted the Nebraska Territorial Legislature to become the first state to give women the vote. "We claim all the rights guaranteed by the Constitution of the United States to citizens of the Republic," said Amelia Bloomer. "We claim to be one-half the people of the United States and we deny the right of the other half to disfranchise us."[1] The Territorial House responded by approving a suffrage bill by a vote of fourteen to eleven. However, Nebraska failed to make history because the legislature adjourned for the year before the upper house acted on it.[2] After Bloomer's speech the *Council Bluffs Chrono-*

type said that while "we may doubt the policy for women to vote but who can draw the line and say that naturally she has not a right to do so?"[3]

Bloomer's speech was the opening salvo in the sixty-year fight that Nebraska women waged to win the vote. They fought unsuccessfully to amend the state constitution and to win referendums in which only men could vote. Top national suffrage leaders debated major newspaper editors on trips to Nebraska, while Clara Bewick Colby, of Beatrice, ran one of the nation's most important suffragist papers. Suffragists also battled anti-suffrage women. Finally, on August 2, 1919, Nebraska ratified the Nineteenth Amendment, granting women the right to vote. But the state battle began with Bloomer, who had attended the original Seneca Falls Convention in 1848 in her hometown and later moved to Council Bluffs.

Amelia Bloomer: The Metro Area's Suffragist Star

When the 1848 Women's Rights Convention adopted a "Womanifesto" that demanded votes for women, it seemed so radical that Bloomer, a temperance advocate, did not sign it. She had attended the meeting at the urging of its organizer, her neighbor Elizabeth Cady Stanton. Stanton launched the battle for suffrage that consumed the rest of her life, after a world antislavery meeting in London had refused to seat women delegates.

Later Bloomer not only signed the Womanifesto but began lecturing on suffrage as well as temperance.[4] She was typical of temperance activists who became suffragists because women had no legal recourse against alcohol-fueled abusive husbands who controlled them, their property, and children.[5]

Bloomer also launched the *Lily*, a newspaper for the Ladies' Temperance Society.[6] Because both Amelia and her husband, Dexter, favored westward expansion, they moved to Ohio, where Amelia continued publishing her paper. After traveling to the western frontier, while Amelia attended a temperance meeting in New York in 1853, Dexter decided that he and Amelia should settle in Council Bluffs, Iowa. Without consulting Amelia, he bought land, ordered a house built, and planned the move.[7] Amelia agreed to move but sold her paper because Council Bluffs was too far from a railroad to distribute it. However, since she continued to lecture, she welcomed the invitation in 1855 to speak to the Nebraska Territorial Legislature.[8] She was one of the nation's first women to address a legislative body.

The Bloomers remained in Council Bluffs for the rest of their lives. Dexter worked in education, and Amelia continued to advocate for women's rights in Iowa, Nebraska, and elsewhere, in addition to working to support the Union during the Civil War. She died in Council Bluffs in 1894 without ever having been allowed to cast a vote.[9] Council Bluffs named the Bloomer School in her honor. In addition, the "bloomers" costume that she abandoned because it was so controversial has kept her name alive. A New York newspaper had picked the name.

A Nebraska State Constitutional Battle

Not only did the territorial legislature fail to give women the vote after Bloomer's speech, but in 1855 Nebraska's territorial constitution—Article II, Section 2—explicitly denied them this right.[10] In 1867, after Nebraska gained statehood, women fought to change this. Stanton and Susan B. Anthony came to Omaha to launch a campaign for suffrage. Two years later the legislature granted women who paid school taxes the right to vote in school elections, making Nebraska the second state to grant school suffrage. Possibly encouraged by this progress, suffragists and their male supporters made expanding suffrage a major issue at the state's 1871 constitutional convention in Lincoln.

Initially, the all-male convention delegates mocked the idea of woman's suffrage. One delegate jokingly suggested giving the vote to women and denying it to men. However, others, such as Douglas County prosecutor Experience Estabrook, took the idea seriously. Estabrook endorsed suffrage because Nebraska gave the vote to all males except infants, the insane, and criminals. Then he asked: "Is she [a woman] an imbecile, is she a lunatic, is she idiotic, is her intellect immature? No, but she is a woman, and not a man . . . I have been told, Mr. President, that it was not the intention at the time of the creation of this earth that woman should belong to the governing power. I want to know, Mr. President, how you found that out?"[11]

Opponents argued that delicate women would wither under exposure to politics. Some said that giving women the vote would destroy marriage.[12] When the convention submitted the proposed constitution and suffrage to voters (all male), both were defeated by a four-to-one margin.[13] Women's rights suffered another setback when married women lost school suffrage in 1875. They regained it six years later, when all Nebraskans with school-age children or who paid taxes on property were allowed to vote in school elections.[14]

A Suffrage Referendum

In 1881 Erasmus Correll of Hebron, Nebraska, sponsored a suffrage bill that the state legislature submitted to voters for approval in 1882, setting off another major battle over the issue. Correll, president of the American Woman Suffrage Association, and his vice president, suffragist publisher Clara Bewick Colby of Beatrice, held the group's 1882 annual convention in Omaha, with Anthony as featured speaker. Two weeks later the National Woman Suffrage Society also met in Omaha. Anthony, the group's acting president, led the event. Interest in suffrage was so high that the number of women's rights groups statewide grew from 39 in 1881 to 175 a year later.[15]

Later that year Anthony returned to Omaha to debate the referendum with *Omaha Bee* editor Edward Rosewater in front of a large crowd at Boyd's Opera House. A few days later, famous Illinois suffragist Phoebe Cousins debated *Omaha Herald* editor Gilbert Hitchcock before another large crowd there.[16] Despite the public excitement, the referendum was defeated by a two-to-one margin.[17]

Aftermath of the Failed Referendum

Following their defeat, Nebraska suffragists retreated, and Anthony declared that from then on she would focus on passage of a national suffrage amendment. In the 1890s state suffragists resumed their battles in the legislature. The country's two major suffrage groups united to form the National American Woman Suffrage Association (NAWSA) in 1890. It held its 1890 convention in Omaha at the home of Omaha's wealthiest couple, George and Sarah Joslyn. Delegates also met with the International Council of Women, which worked for women's causes worldwide. Both Anthony and Stanton attended these meetings.[18] However, Nebraska did not again consider changing its constitution to allow women the right to vote until 1914.

A 1914 Proposed State Amendment

By 1914 all of Nebraska's neighboring states had granted women the vote. However, the Democratic Party, the liquor interests, and the state's large German American community opposed giving women the franchise, and the National Brewers Association spent large sums opposing suffrage. Many Catholic and Lutheran German Americans opposed suffrage in part because they thought it endangered traditional family values.[19]

Some women opposed suffrage because they thought that it would cost women the status they enjoyed as wives and mothers. They feared that it would cause men to deny women economic support, increase divorce rates, and force women into the labor force. They also feared that women voters would support unions, reformers, socialists, communists, and anarchists. The Wage Earner's League, made up of about five hundred secretaries, teachers, and clerks, also opposed suffrage for fear of a negative impact on their jobs.[20]

Omaha mayor James Dahlman and political boss Tom Denison opposed suffrage because they believed it threatened Omaha's brewing industry and the alcohol, gambling, and prostitution operations on which their machine depended. Dahlman became the anti-suffragists' spokesman.[21] Immigrant Omaha men also opposed suffrage because of its ties to temperance. In many of their cultures drinking was routine, and then as now, Omaha had numerous bars.

The anti-suffrage forces organized the Nebraska Association Opposed to Woman Suffrage at a 1914 meeting at the Omaha home of Mrs. E. P. Peck, who became the association's president. The group was especially active in Omaha and Lincoln, where it raised funds through teas, luncheons, and balls. It also formed junior auxiliaries at colleges and educated the public through speeches, literature, and advertising.[22] A men's anti-suffrage group also fought against suffrage on moral grounds. For example, it distributed a message to Catholic men titled "Lest Catholic Men Be Misled," written by Mary Nash Crofoot of Omaha, a prominent Catholic.[23]

Proponents of suffrage included the state's suffrage and temperance associations and both the Nebraska Federation of Labor and the Omaha Central Labor Union.[24] Jane Addams of Chicago's famous Hull House spoke in Omaha in favor of suffrage.[25] Other supporters included about three-fourths of Omaha's three thousand African American voters. African American supporters held several meetings at the home of Cecilia Jewell.[26] Jewell was a noted singer and, with her husband, James, owned the Jewell Building on North Twenty-Fourth Street, where many of the nation's top African American musicians performed. These efforts failed. The all-male electorate again defeated suffrage two to one.[27]

An Omaha-Born Suffragist Confronts President Wilson

While Nebraskans were debating suffrage at home, Omaha native Rheta Childe Dorr confronted U.S. president Woodrow Wilson over the proposed federal suffrage amendment at an event she had organized to win media attention for the cause.

In 1914 Dorr, forty-seven, led a delegation of five hundred socially prominent club women wearing white suffrage dresses into the White House to demand that Wilson support the federal suffrage amendment. The Congressional Union for Woman Suffrage, a new and more aggressive suffrage organization, of which Dorr was a member, was promoting the amendment instead of state-by-state actions.[28]

Dorr had become a suffragist at the age of twelve, when she sneaked out of her parents' Omaha home to attend a suffragist rally. Her parents learned that she had joined the Woman Suffrage Association by reading her name on a list of new members in the newspaper the next day. She left Nebraska as a young woman to pursue journalistic and suffragist causes, becoming the first editor of the *Suffragist*, the Congressional Union's official organ.[29]

President Wilson normally refused to meet with suffragists, but he had invited these upper-class women into the White House and was surprised when Dorr confronted him. She questioned his opposition to the national amendment—he regarded suffrage as a state issue. She noted that although the 1912 Democratic Party platform (written in Baltimore) did not endorse the amendment, circumstances had changed, and Wilson had endorsed other issues not endorsed in the platform.

"Mr. President, you said you did this thing because changed conditions warranted changed policies. We agree with you and we are here to tell you how importantly the whole woman suffrage situation has changed since the Baltimore Platform was written and how changed action is called for," Dorr said. She reminded Wilson that in 1914, 3.6 million women voted in nine states instead of four states, like when he was elected in 1912.

She asked for his immediate action, but Wilson refused, saying that he would not interfere with the process under which each state determined suffrage. The two battled back and forth until Wilson lost patience and told Dorr "I think that it is not proper for me to stand here and be cross-examined by you." Then he abruptly left, shaking no hands as he had planned.[30]

As Dorr had hoped, newspapers, including the *New York Times*, covered the event, sparking the public controversy that she had sought and more genteel suffragists feared. Wilson did nothing to promote suffrage until he finally endorsed the Nineteenth Amendment at the end of World War I in recognition of the contributions of women to the war effort.[31]

Doris Stevens

Another Omaha native, Central High School alum Doris Stevens, who had left the city as a young woman, became a leader of the militant National Woman's Party organized by Alice Paul. She was arrested for picketing at the White House in 1917 and served three days of her sixty-day sentence in a workhouse before being pardoned. She also was arrested at a demonstration at New York's Metropolitan Opera House in 1919 and published the book *Jailed for Freedom* in 1920. She remained active in working for feminist causes throughout her life.[32]

Winning the Vote

In Nebraska suffrage remained a contentious issue to the end. In 1917 the Nebraska Legislature approved a limited suffrage law that seemingly was nullified by a referendum petition drive. A

VOTES FOR OMAHA WOMEN

complicated battle involving the legality of the petitions ensued. However, in 1919 the state supreme court declared the petitions fraudulent. Nebraska ratified the Nineteenth Amendment in 1919, and Nebraska women finally won full suffrage when the amendment took effect in 1920.[33] Four years later Nebraska elected three women to the old two-house legislature, including Mabel Gillespie of Gretna, the first woman to cover a news beat at the *Omaha Bee*. She was reelected four years later. In 1944 she was the first women to run as a major party candidate for Congress. A Democrat, she lost to Howard Buffett, father of Warren Buffett.[34]

Since Suffrage

A century after gaining suffrage, Nebraska women today serve as judges, mayors, school board members, county commissioners, and state senators. Long gone are the days when the Unicameral had only one or two women members.

In 1986 Republican Kay Orr defeated Democrat Helen Boosalis in one of the nation's first all-woman governor's races, and in 2021 Omaha and Lincoln both had women mayors, while one of the state's two U.S. senators was a woman. With more potential female than male voters coupled with a growing interest in running for office at all levels, the involvement of Nebraska women in politics is only likely to increase.

5

Prostitution in Wide-Open Omaha

During the Gilded Age, Omaha was a wide-open river town where prostitution, gambling, and other vices flourished, especially in downtown's "Burnt District." Owners of brothels paid graft to the city's political machine, and madams like Anna Wilson amassed fortunes. In the process, however, they exploited thousands of local women, who paid a terrible price for working in "the world's oldest profession."

Ironically, prostitution flourished most openly during the Victorian era and the decades that followed, when society restricted the activities of respectable women to protect their virtue. Omahans largely turned a blind eye to the exploitation of poor women, who regularly turned to prostitution because of the terrible wages other jobs paid. *Omaha World-Herald* columnist Elia Peattie was among the few to decry the double standard of condemning women but not the men who paid them.

Screams, curses, and protests rang out in downtown Omaha brothels as drunken young society men attending a turn-of-the-century political event or convention descended on the city's numerous houses of ill repute. "They are drunk, we fear them. WE NEVER GET OVER THIS FEAR although we have seen the same performance daily year after year," wrote Josie Washburn, one of Omaha's top madams, who later turned against her trade in her 1909 book, *The Underworld Sewer.* "A drunken bunch has arrived, they are young and handsome fellows, they use vile language. . . . They are society dudes and imagining they are making a hit with our girls by exhibiting their toughness, and failing to find an appreciative audience, they pinch and hurt the girls just to hear them scream, and curse and call them names."[1]

In 1910 Omaha was home to about twenty-six hundred prostitutes, according to possibly dubious census data.[2] The number of brothels rose from seventeen in 1880 to more than one hundred in 1910.[3] Underground tunnels connected downtown hotels with the brothels and gambling houses.[4] Most were located in the so-called Burnt District between Douglas, Cass, Sixteenth Street, and the Missouri River.[5] As long as prostitutes paid their protection fees, police made few arrests.

The Cribs

Conditions were especially sordid in the easily visible Cribs, small units on brightly lit alleys in the Arcade, a square block bounded by Eighth, Ninth, and Dodge Streets and Capitol Avenue.[6] "Each crib consists of two small rooms about six feet high. . . . The alleys are paved, regardless of expense, and have heavy iron gates," wrote Washburn. "One of these alleys is covered by a fancy roof, the ceiling has a showy red design, embellished with many electric lights."[7] The bright lights attracted crowds of men, including high school boys. Women, many just teenagers, paid owner E. F. Martin from one to five dollars a day in rent plus a fifty-dollar key fee. If they failed to pay the daily rent, he threw their belongings into the street.[8]

"The girls who occupy the crib are always under the influence of a lover who fleeces them of all money above their bare living expenses," wrote Washburn. "Some of these girls with their pretty faces seem so young and frail as to be mere children. . . . They do not even realize they are in the worst of slavery."[9]

Women fell into prostitution often as a result of male deception as well as poverty and abuse.[10] Some single mothers became prostitutes because they could not make enough money from other available jobs, like domestic work, to keep their children out of orphanages.[11] In the 1850s, for example, three-quarters of prostitutes were former household servants or seamstresses whose wages weren't enough to provide a living.[12]

The Omaha cribs owner Martin controlled an additional 140 to 150 prostitutes in his various houses and collected about $75,000 a year in rent and fees from the women, equivalent to more than $1.8 million today.[13] A 1907 *Omaha World-Herald* exposé led city prosecutors to shut the cribs down, despite the regular protection that Martin paid to "Boss" Tom Dennison, head of Omaha's political machine. However, he continued to operate his other houses for several more years.[14]

Other leaders of the vice industry included Omaha's most famous madam, Anna Wilson, who shares an elaborate tomb in Prospect Hill Cemetery with her gambler boyfriend, Dan Allen.

Anna Wilson

To her contemporaries Wilson was "a woman of mystery," according to historian Alfred Sorenson.[15] Thanks to modern Memorial Day festivities at Prospect Hill, she is one of the best-known local women of her era—a key figure in a dark business who left her fortune to charity. In gratitude a prominent Omaha woman annually laid a wreath on her grave, a tradition the modern celebration has revived.

Accounts of Wilson's life differ, but she was likely born in Georgia in 1835, the daughter of a Baptist preacher. An uncle raised her after her parents died.[16] She apparently moved to New Orleans at an unknown date. There she met Dan Allen, who persuaded her to come to Omaha in 1867.

"I just happened here," she told the *Daily News* in 1911. "I was roaming at the time and thought Omaha would be a good place." She went to work in Allen's gambling house and became his companion until he died thirteen years later.[17]

By 1886 Wilson had earned enough in "retail services" to open a red brick twenty-five-room mansion with bay windows at Ninth and Douglas. It had forty-six beds and columns of carved naked women on the stone front porch.[18] Wilson would not accept girls new to prostitution into her house. She also paid their medical expenses to combat venereal disease and funeral expenses for those who committed suicide.[19] She encouraged her women to marry and get out of prostitution if they could.[20]

Allen and Wilson lived colorfully and extravagantly. In 1875 they were victims of a notorious theft. Wilson had dressed up lavishly in diamonds for a masquerade ball, got drunk on champagne, and was taken home in a hackney. When she woke up the next morning, her diamonds were gone. Allen fingered the culprit and threatened him with jail unless he returned the jewels. The man returned the stolen diamonds, but Allen reneged on the deal and reported the crime to police, resulting in prison for the thief.[21]

When Allen died, in 1884, Wilson marked his grave with an elaborate monument in Prospect Hill that she visited and decorated with fresh flowers almost daily.[22] After she left prostitution in the 1890s, she lived quietly in a house at 2018 Wirt Street and invested in real estate deals that made up about half of her fortune. She also gave generously to charities.[23]

Her offer of her old brothel to the city was controversial, but the city rented it from her for $125 a month for use as a hospital and took ownership of the building in 1911, after Wilson died. The city was quick to remove the naked women columns from the front porch, replacing them with more respectable plain wood columns.[24] Eventually, the hospital became a venereal disease clinic.

At the same time that Wilson offered her house to the city, she also announced her plan to spread her fortune among Omaha charities because she was seventy-six, had no heirs, and had only months to live.[25] Her beneficiaries included Creche Home for Children and Prospect Hill Cemetery.[26]

In gratitude for her support of the Creche day nursery, Mrs. Thomas L. Kimball, mother of architect Thomas R. Kimball, began laying a wreath on Wilson's tomb every Memorial Day, and her son continued the tradition. The practice ceased with Kimball's death in 1934. It was resumed in the 1970s, after *Omaha World-Herald* columnist Robert McMorris wrote about Wilson. Now the wreath laying highlights the Prospect Hill Memorial Day celebration.[27]

Many modern downtown landmarks—including TD Ameritrade Park, Lewis & Clark Landing, CHI Health Center, and the Bob Kerrey Pedestrian Bridge—are located on or near Wilson's old properties.[28]

Josie Washburn

Omaha's second most famous madam, Josie Washburn, turned against her occupation and exposed its evils in her book, *The Underworld Sewer*. Like Wilson, her origins are mysterious, but she seems to have been born in 1853, possibly in Rhode Island, Maine, or Wisconsin. Her real name might have been Helena; prostitutes often used aliases and created fictitious life stories.

After arriving in Omaha at age seventeen, she worked for Wilson for eight years and often appeared in police court records on prostitution charges.[29] In July 1879 she shot herself, and the arrests ceased. A story in the *Omaha Herald* said a firearm that she was handling accidentally discharged, and she carried the bullet in her shoulder for the rest of her life.[30] Washburn disappeared for fifteen years, then reappeared in Nebraska, claiming she had been married and that her husband had deserted her. There are no public records of a marriage, though. Single and caught up in the depression of the 1890s, she opened a brothel in Lincoln. In 1906 she and six other brothel keepers sued the Lincoln police chief and a city detective for blackmail, but the officers were acquitted.[31]

Washburn then retired from prostitution, moved back to Omaha, and in 1909 published her exposé. *The Underworld Sewer* had little immediate impact on prostitution in Omaha, and Washburn was largely forgotten until the University of Nebraska Press reissued her book in 1997.[32] According to some accounts, Washburn moved to Minneapolis and then to Spokane, Washington, where she was lost to history.[33]

Today Wilson and Washburn have become almost cult figures in Omaha. The Wilson and Washburn Bar at Fourteenth and Harney Streets is named for them and decorated with haunting photos of prostitutes like those who staffed their brothels in the era when the building was constructed. These vacant-eyed photos are a grim reminder that the lives of Omaha prostitutes were nothing like Wilson's.

Life in the Prostitution Industry

Midwestern railroad and river cities such as Omaha, Chicago, St. Joseph (Missouri), and Kansas City were magnets for prostitutes. Many traveled on a regional circuit that included these communities as well as St. Paul, Minnesota, and Sioux City, Iowa. This gave customers variety if they tired of the local prostitutes, according to Bristow.[34]

Omaha's unwritten code divided the city into zones of virtue and vice. Some Omahans felt that prostitution helped protect "good" women from sexual assault but that prostitutes were fair game for rapists. It was presumed that all sex with them was consensual, and men were never convicted of raping a prostitute.[35] Prostitutes could not walk the streets during the day and could eat and shop only in restricted locations. Martin required prostitutes employed in the Arcade to buy their food and alcohol from one of his associates who owned a nearby saloon and a restaurant. After automobiles were invented, one madam hired cars to give her employees rides several times a week.[36] When women got the vote, political bosses required madams and their employees to vote and contribute to campaigns.[37]

Sometimes prostitutes were arrested and the madams fined, but most soon returned to work. Citizens formed committees decrying prostitution because prostitutes were frequently involved in thefts and disorderly conduct. Their customers were never arrested, however, and police and other officials continued making money, as did property owners in the vice district.[38] In 1911 the city closed some of the most disorderly brothels, but many of the women who had worked in them became streetwalkers, and a number of madams relocated their establishments.[39]

A Woman Columnist's View of Prostitution

Although much of respectable Omaha seemingly ignored prostitution, *Omaha World-Herald* columnist Elia Peattie excoriated men for exploiting prostitutes and society for failing to forgive "fallen women." "I know of a girl 14 years of age who this week found the shelter of an Open Door," she wrote. "The man who ruined her was over twice her age. The girl has been placed in the Milford home where she has been cared for physically and morally and taught a trade so that when she leaves, she will not have to join the ranks of the unhappy sisterhood."[40]

Peattie recalled a sermon by a self-righteous minister who denounced prostitutes but did not criticize their customers. In contrast, she blamed the "brutality of man" for the "downfall of woman, and not any innate viciousness in the woman herself," writing, "I will admit that anyone who sees a company of these fallen women together in 'the cage' at the city jail, swearing, jeering and laughing with a gaiety more dreadful than any grief, will find it difficult to believe that they were ever pure."

Peattie lamented that economic necessity often led women into such a fate and added, "I could weep for the curse that curses women and which never seems to rest on man."[41] Peattie's column appeared in 1894, fifteen years before the city cracked down on prostitution.

Aftermath

Although the cribs, brothels, and underground tunnels from downtown hotels to vice establishments are gone, Omaha still battles prostitution, now often called human trafficking or (if voluntary) sex work. Women use the internet to connect with "Johns," and occasionally a prominent man will be caught in a police sting. During annual events such as the College World Series, social service agencies alert hotels to the signs of trafficking and organized prostitution rings, but the battle never ends.

On a personal note, Peattie's comment about seeing the prostitutes locked up in the city jail evoked memories of covering similar conditions in the old municipal jail in the 1970s. Catcalls and curses greeted me and my police escort as women banged on their cell doors. They still wore their streetwalker clothes. The un-air-conditioned jail, which has since been torn down, sweltered in the July heat.

The scene haunted me for weeks as it apparently did Peattie. Like her, I asked, where were their Johns? How much has really changed since the wide-open era? Crime Stoppers' rewards program now offers significant cash awards to anonymous callers whose tips lead to the arrest of sex traffickers.[42]

6

Health Care

After the Civil War, Omaha churchwomen, including Catholic nuns and Lutheran deaconesses, opened the first local hospitals and nursing schools. They turned nursing into the second largest profession for educated women, and a few Gilded Age women became physicians as they began insisting on equal educational and employment opportunities.[1] This chapter tells these stories by profiling some of the most important women in nursing and medicine, including the local nursing educators who enhanced their field's status.

Nursing Sisters at Work

Elia Peattie, of the *Omaha World-Herald*, took her readers behind the scenes at St. Joseph Hospital in 1891 to showcase the work and dedication of its nursing sisters, writing:

> Sisters assist in the work of the physicians. Some of them are indeed fitted for bold surgery and there is one Sister now at the hospital who can take up an artery as well as a physician. Their nursing is skillful—they know what to do in every emergency. They can care for a man in the crisis of pneumonia or take one through the run of typhoid fever and its dangerous convalesce; they do not need assistance in midwifery and they know every device for mitigating suffer-

ing. . . . Their steps are noiseless, their voices are low, their bodies capable of great endurance.

Not only did the nursing sisters work twelve-hour shifts; they did all their own cleaning, cooking, and laundry. The nuns welcomed people of all races and religions. They spoke "gentle words" and performed "gentle deeds." They left Peattie humbled. "To say that I felt secular is putting it mildly. I felt actually profane and was relieved when I got out among people just as frivolous, as selfish and heedless as I was myself."[2]

Opening Hospitals

Protestant churchwomen and Catholic nuns opened Omaha's first two hospitals, Clarkson and St. Joseph's, in 1869–70. A few years later Lutheran deaconesses, professional church workers who lived in the community and served the needy, played a major role in starting Immanuel Hospital. Still later, the Sisters of Mercy opened St. Catherine's Hospital, ancestor of Bergan Mercy Medical Center. At all institutions female nurses provided most of the bedside care, and no hospital could have operated without its women employees.

Clarkson Hospital

In 1869 women of several Protestant denominations organized Good Samaritan Hospital, ancestor of the modern Clarkson Hospital; it opened a year later at Twenty-Fourth and Webster Streets.[3] By the next year, however, the volunteer board of women asked Episcopal bishop Robert Clarkson to convert it into a diocesan institution because administering the hospital was too demanding. Good Samaritan was renamed in Clarkson's honor and remained part of the Episcopal Diocese of Nebraska until 1965, when it became independent.[4] In 1998 it merged with the University of Nebraska Medical Center (UNMC).

In 1888 Bishop Clarkson's wife, Meliora, worked with deaconesses from Trinity Episcopal Cathedral to start Nebraska's first
nurses training school. Ten years later Meliora Clarkson founded
a children's hospital, and the deaconesses became some of the
first caregivers.[5]

St. Joseph's Hospital

In 1870, a year after Good Samaritan was organized, Bishop James
O'Gorman asked the Sisters of Mercy to run the new St. Joseph's
Mercy Hospital at Twelfth and Mason Streets. The $10,000 two-
story frame building included two wards and ten rooms.[6] The
sisters traveled all over Nebraska on Union Pacific trains solicit-
ing funds for the much-needed facility serving Omaha's sixteen
thousand residents. Over the next decade St. Joseph's treated
fifteen hundred patients.[7]

The hospital developed financial problems, however, because
there were not enough Mercy Sisters to run both the hospital and
their numerous schools. They sold St. Joseph's to the Poor Sisters
of St. Francis in 1880.[8] Sarah Emily and John Creighton contributed heavily to building a new, larger hospital at Tenth and Castelar Streets that opened in 1892. After Sarah Emily died, it was
renamed Creighton Memorial St. Joseph's Hospital in her honor.[9]

That year Creighton's new medical college moved into the old
hospital, and St. Joseph's became the university's teaching hospital.[10] St. Joseph's eventually opened a nursing school for lay
students that was affiliated with Creighton. When its first class
graduated in 1920, the nurses received their diplomas during
Creighton's commencement ceremonies.[11]

Immanuel Hospital

In 1890 the Reverend E. A. Fogelstrom, pastor of Immanuel
Lutheran Church, created Immanuel Hospital and Deaconess
Motherhouse to serve North Omaha's growing Swedish pop-

ulation. Fogelstrom sent them to Philadelphia and Sweden for training until he could educate them in Omaha.

The deaconesses opened the Immanuel Deaconess Home for the aged and infirm at Thirty-Fourth and Fowler Streets and expanded into other services, including a general hospital.[12]

St. Catherine's Hospital

The Sisters of Mercy returned to health care in 1910, when Bishop Richard Scannell asked them to open St. Catherine's Hospital for maternity care. Eventually, St. Catherine's, at 810 Forrest Street, expanded into a general hospital and ran a nursing school that was also affiliated with Creighton.[13] St. Catherine's was the predecessor of Bergan Mercy Medical Center, which has become Creighton's modern medical center and teaching hospital.

By the early 1900s women had laid the groundwork for modern Omaha's health care system by opening hospitals and establishing the nursing schools that gave local hospitals well-educated nurses.

Nursing

By the end of the nineteenth century, nursing had become the second largest career field for educated women after teaching. Early nurses were revered for their dedication to sick people, but doctors often treated them as subordinates rather than colleagues, a number of nurses said.

Some of this was sexism because doctors were overwhelmingly male and nurses were virtually all women. However, it also reflected the gap in academic preparation between the two fields. Before the modern women's movement, most nurses graduated from hospital programs that did not grant bachelor's degrees. A revolution in nursing education nationally and locally that began during the 1960s upgraded nursing education, leading to improvements in pay and professional status.

Three Omaha nursing educators, Dr. Barbara Braden of Creighton and Dr. Rena Boyle of the University of Nebraska College of Nursing, and Professor Dorothy Patach, of the University of Nebraska at Omaha, made major local contributions to these changes.

Dr. Barbara Braden

The traditional submissive role of nurses did not suit internationally acclaimed nursing educator Dr. Barbara Braden, dean emeritus of Creighton's Graduate School. Braden, a native of Griswold, Iowa, near Omaha, created the Braden Scale to assess pressure sores in bedridden patients that is widely used in American hospitals and nursing homes and has been translated into several languages.[14] She has lectured on it nationally and internationally.

Braden began teaching nursing after earning one of Creighton's first bachelor's degrees in nursing in 1967. Until the shift to the more demanding bachelor's degree, physicians tended to be "mostly dismissive of nurses." Braden said, "I can remember being in a multi-disciplinary meeting at Creighton where some doctors said they didn't consider nurses to be too smart."[15] By the 1970s Creighton nursing professors were required to have master's degrees, and today most of them have doctorates, like faculty in other disciplines.

Braden received her master's degree from the University of California at San Francisco in 1975 and her doctorate from the University of Texas at Austin in 1988. She taught nursing at Creighton from 1975 to 1994, rising from instructor to full professor. She was named dean of the Graduate School in 1995, a position she held until she retired in 2006. She has received numerous awards and continued to lecture after her retirement.

Dr. Rena Boyle

During the same years Dr. Rena Boyle greatly expanded and upgraded nursing education at the University of Nebraska

Medical Center. Boyle, who received her bachelor's, master's, and doctoral degrees in nursing from the University of Minnesota, joined UNMC in 1967 and became the first dean of the College of Nursing when its status was upgraded from a school in 1968.[16]

Boyle, who retired in 1979 and died in 2006, created both a master's degree and associate degree programs in nursing, in addition to establishing off-campus programs that allowed nurses to upgrade their RN degrees to bachelor's degrees. Through this innovative "learning continuum," nurses could advance in their field and helped Nebraska meet its need for nurses with varying educational and skill levels. Nursing College enrollment grew from under one hundred to more than seven hundred. Boyle also served as a consultant to the surgeon general for the U.S. and numerous other nursing programs.[17]

Professor Dorothy Patach

Patach, who grew up in South Omaha, originally wanted to be a doctor but became a nurse because that's what women did in the 1940s. After receiving her degree from the Nebraska School of Nursing in 1944, she eventually earned a BS in nutrition and an MS in nursing education from the University of Omaha. During her long career, which combined operating room nursing with teaching, she helped build nursing education programs in Omaha and Council Bluffs.[18]

In 1959 the University of Omaha hired Patach to lead its Nursing Program. She advised students, directed allied health education, and worked with the dean of the College of Arts and Sciences. During the 1960s she persuaded the university to allow women to wear slacks, arguing to Chancellor Milo Bail they were an alternative to miniskirts.

Patach also was an environmentalist who fought dumping in South Omaha's ravines and other open areas. The Dorothy Patach

Environmental Area at Twentieth and N Streets, across the street from her childhood home, is named for her.[19]

Nursing Becomes a Chosen Career

Today students of both genders pursue nursing careers because they like the field, not because they can't become doctors, said Braden. "I think many are attracted to the emotional part of nursing. They like having closer contact with people to better serve them." Nursing also requires fewer years of study and offers more flexible hours and family-friendly careers than being a doctor.[20]

Today's physicians have a greater appreciation for the role of nurses, Braden said. In addition, more nurses have advanced degrees and specialize in fields such as nurse practitioner that give them more independence and better pay.[21]

Women Physicians

Despite gender barriers in getting into medical school, there were more early women physicians than lawyers in Omaha and elsewhere. "Medicine was one of the first professional fields to attract woman when her emancipation from home duties only began to be agitated," according to a history of medicine in Nebraska.[22] In 1883 Dr. Georgia Arbuckle Fix, who practiced near North Platte, became the first woman graduate of the Omaha Medical College, predecessor of the University of Nebraska College of Medicine.[23]

Dr. Amelia Burroughs, a homeopath who moved from Council Bluffs, Iowa, in 1883, was Omaha's first woman physician. A year later Dr. Gertrude Jones Cuscaden and Dr. Mary J. Breckenridge also began practicing in Omaha. By the end of the decade Omaha had four additional women physicians.[24]

Even before the women's movement, Omaha produced a number of notable female physicians, including one of the first doctors on the staff of Methodist Hospital and a doctor who won international awards for her work with refugees after World War I.

Dr. Mary Breckenridge

Dr. Breckenridge, who became one of the first thirteen physicians on the staff of Methodist Hospital in 1891, didn't even study medicine until she was forty and had had six children, the youngest who was only two at the time. She had followed a more typical path of becoming a teacher and marrying her husband, Charles, an attorney, when she was just eighteen. Although she was from Ohio, she studied medicine at Hahnemann College in Chicago while her oldest daughter cared for her toddler. She graduated with honors in 1883, and a year later the family moved to Omaha, where Charles became a prominent attorney. Mary built a large practice and was acclaimed for her "wonderful character and personality."

In 1900 the *Medical Visitor* publication saluted Breckinridge and other women physicians in the era's flowery prose: "They are not only physicians but more than that they are endowed with woman's winsome ways and gentleness and kindliness of heart. . . . We doubt that judging from the pictures, if another city in the Union has as handsome a faculty of women physicians as does Omaha." After Charles became ill, Mary gave up her practice to accompany him to California. She died in Tacoma, Washington, in 1924.[25]

While Dr. Breckinridge was nontraditional in entering medicine at midlife, her career was mundane compared with that of Dr. Olga Stastny, who became famous for her work in post–World War I refugee camps.

Dr. Olga Stastny

Stastny, a native of Wilber, Nebraska, received international acclaim for directing a hospital for Greek refugees fleeing Turkish persecution after World War I. She had married her husband, Charles, a dentist, as a teenager and entered medical school a year after his death in 1907.

When Stastny enrolled at the University of Nebraska College of Medicine, she was the only woman in her class. She graduated in 1913, when she was thirty-five. After interning in Boston, she returned to practice in Omaha.[26]

During World War I Stastny joined the Red Cross because the U.S. Army refused to commission women doctors. The Red Cross sent her to France after the war to care for war victims. While there, she met the daughter of the president of Czechoslovakia, who persuaded her to move to Prague to lecture teenage girls about their femininity and living a clean moral life.[27] Stastny's fluency in Czech made her highly effective.

After her son died in an airplane crash in 1921, while he was touring Czechoslovakia, she returned to the United States and toured the Midwest, speaking on her overseas experiences. However, she returned to Europe in 1923 as medical director of a women's hospital on Macronissi Island, Greece, that cared for thousands of Christian Greek refugees fleeing Turkish persecution.[28] The head of the American Women's Hospitals called Stastny the "heroine of the hour," and the Greek government awarded her the Cross of Saint George.

Later that year she returned to Omaha and reestablished her obstetrics and gynecology practice as well as joining the faculty of the University of Nebraska College of Medicine.[29] She ended her career as the medical director for the Supreme Forest Woodmen Circle Insurance Company and died in 1952.[30]

Although women could become famous physicians like Dr. Stastny and could set up family medical practices if they were married to physicians, that didn't mean that society treated the two partners equally. The story of the couple who founded the old Doctor's Hospital shows this disparity.

Physician Couples: Not Quite Equal

Although Dr. Lillian Nuckolls and her husband, Dr. Albert Condon, were medical partners, their obituaries illustrate the unequal
status of female doctors. In 1912 the couple founded, owned, and
operated the Nicholas Senn Hospital at 501 Park Avenue, renamed
Doctor's Hospital when it was reorganized in 1916.[31] When Condon died, in 1939, his hometown paper, the *Indianapolis Star*,
ran an Associated Press story describing his education, medical
specialty, and career.[32]

In contrast, when Nuckolls died a year later, the *Omaha World-
Herald* reported that "Mrs. Lillian Condon, 68, died last night
at the Nicholas Senn Hospital that she had owned and operated
with her husband." The second paragraph stated that like her
husband, she was a physician, known to medical professionals as
Dr. Lillian Nuckolls. The story referred to her as "Mrs.," rather
than "Dr.," and did not mention her education or medical specialty.[33] However, a registry of graves says she was born in Auburn,
Illinois, in 1871, and other scattered online sources indicate she
did her residency at the Illinois Hospital for the Insane in Jack-
sonville, then moved to Glenwood, Iowa, near Omaha, in 1903.

To a modern reader, such treatment seems disrespectful, but
the women's movement, and physicians like Dr. Muriel Frank,
helped break the local glass ceiling in medicine in the 1970s. Frank,
a tiny but forceful anesthesiologist, became the first woman president of the Metropolitan Omaha Medical Society.

Dr. Muriel Frank

Women physicians remained a minority in their field until the
women's movement of the 1970s, when a large number of women
began studying medicine. Established physicians like Dr. Muriel
Frank, who helped start the anesthesiology department at Methodist Hospital, encouraged and mentored them.

Frank received a "Shattered Ceiling" award from the Omaha League of Women Voters in 1995 for her contributions to gender equality and for paving the way for hundreds of women physicians. "She was always ready to mentor the other women in the medical field," said Dr. Michelle Knolla, a past president of the Metropolitan Omaha Medical Society.[34]

As a teenager, Frank, a 1935 graduate of Central High School, became determined to study medicine, despite the obstacles she encountered.[35] "The dean did not want women in medical school, and it was a challenge for her to get in," said her son, Dr. James Steinberg, an infectious disease specialist at Emory University in Atlanta. "She was driven to succeed in medicine. She had to work harder and be better."[36]

Frank received her MD degree from the University of Nebraska in 1943, one of two women in her class. After interning in St. Louis and at Bellevue Hospital in New York, she returned to Omaha in 1947 and co-founded Methodist's anesthesiology department. She headed the department for fifteen years, supervising a mostly male staff. She also was on the clinical faculty at the University of Nebraska Medical Center.[37]

Frank married her husband, Dr. Maurice "Moe" Steinberg, a urologist, in 1950, which helped keep her in Omaha. "If she hadn't met him, she might have left Omaha," said Steinberg. He described his four-foot-eleven mother as a tough woman who routinely worked twelve-hour days, never took a sick day, and was on call every other night. "She would leave home earlier and come home later than my father." She was late for dinner most evenings because she took extra time to answer questions from the patients scheduled for surgery the next day, Steinberg said. Her husband usually cooked.

"She was not emotional, although I think she felt guilty that she was not around as much as some mothers," he said. "She was a firm believer that a woman should do what her talents and skills led her to. She was tough on some women and would tell them that they had to be tougher. She was more like a drill sergeant than a compassionate consoler. She had a commanding presence."[38]

In 1989 Frank became the first woman president of the local medical society, an office her husband had held in 1974. It was the first time nationally that a husband and wife had each headed their local medical society.[39]

Steinberg noted that when his mother became a doctor, the field of medicine was very hierarchical, and nurses were expected to take orders. That role would not have suited Dr. Muriel Frank, who worked tirelessly as a physician into her seventies. She died in 2020.[40]

Women in Today's Health Care

Television commercials for today's Omaha hospitals feature women working as physicians, nurses, and various types of technicians and therapists. About half the students in most medical school classes are women, and more men are studying nursing.

Groundbreaking women in both nursing and medicine helped create these changes, building on the legacy of the women who founded many of Omaha's hospitals, transformed local nursing education, and opened careers as doctors to females.

1. Women dominated the first Omaha High School classes, including these members of the first graduating class in 1876. Courtesy of Omaha Central High Journalism Department and Central High School Foundation Register Archives website.

2. A bequest from Mary Lucretia Creighton established the university in 1878. Courtesy of Creighton University.

3. Anna Wilson, Omaha's most famous madam. Courtesy of Tom Kerr.

4. These three young members of the Omaha Tribe participated in the Indian Congress of the Trans-Mississippi Exposition in 1898. From the collection of the Omaha Public Library.

5. In 1914 Omaha native Rheta Childe Dorr
confronted President Woodrow Wilson over
suffrage. Library of Congress.

6. Sarah Joslyn created and funded Joslyn Art Museum. Courtesy of Legacy Preservation.

7. A Sister of Mercy teaching future nurses at St. Catherine's Hospital School of Nursing. Sisters of Mercy.

8. Nuns were assigned large classes like this one at St. Peter's Elementary School in 1948. Sisters of Mercy.

9. Rachel Gallagher, with Creighton University leaders Carl Reinert, SJ, and Henry Linn, SJ, was best known for her work with the city parks in the postwar era. Courtesy of Creighton University.

10. Mabel Criss bought the insurance agency that became Mutual of Omaha. Courtesy of Creighton University.

11. Mildred Brown and John Markoe, sj, were early Omaha civil rights leaders. They worked together on civil rights beginning in the 1940s. Courtesy of Creighton University.

12. Elizabeth Pittman was Creighton's first African American female law graduate. Pittman graduated in 1948. Courtesy of Creighton University.

13. Emmy Gifford was an artist but best known for her work in children's theater. Photo used with permission of the *Omaha World-Herald*.

14. Nebraska Furniture Mart founder Rose "Mrs. B" Blumkin on her scooter. Courtesy of the Rose Blumkin collection at the Nebraska Jewish Historical Society.

15. Betty Abbott, after her 1965 election, was the
first and only woman on the Omaha City Council
during her years at city hall. Photo used with
permission of the *Omaha World-Herald*.

16. Dr. Muriel Frank was the first woman president of the Metropolitan Omaha Medical Society. Courtesy of Metropolitan Omaha Medical Society.

17. Softball coach Mary Higgins helped start Creighton women's sports. Higgins became softball coach in 1975. Courtesy of Creighton University.

18. Bertha Calloway founded the Great
Plains Black History Museum in 1976, now
located in the Jewell Building. Courtesy of
the Great Plains Black History Museum.

19. Janice Stoney, first woman member of the Aksarben Board of Governors, with her husband, Larry. Courtesy of Janice Stoney.

20. Dr. Gail Walling Yanney helped found the Omaha Women's Fund in 1990. Courtesy of Gail Walling Yanney.

7

Human Services

From the first, women dominated human services delivery in Omaha because nurturing and volunteering have long been considered women's work. Early churchwomen started services for poor families, children, and young working women because there was no government safety net. Immigrant and minority women cared for people in their communities even though they were poor themselves. Rich women, who seldom worked outside the home until the women's movement of the 1970s, often turned volunteer work into a substitute for paid careers.

Ironically, the city's best-known human services agency is Boys Town, where unsung women, especially nuns, cared for the boys for decades while men made the decisions. Women also raised much of the money.

Beginning in the early 1970s, Omaha engaged in a sort of gender-driven tug of war over human services. Young women began advocating for equal funding for female programs. Women who joined boards found that they had the clout to create these services because many men were less hostile to these needs than unaware of them.

Women Found Human Services

In the 1870s Edward Creighton gave his wife, Mary Lucretia, about twenty-five dollars a day to distribute to the needy, an example of how they got help before the government social safety net existed. Nurturing and volunteering were traditionally considered "women's work," said Michael Mclarney, retired executive director of United Way. In the era before Social Security and government welfare services, charities sponsored by religious and rich women were among the few sources of help.[1]

By the 1870s local Protestant women such as Mrs. J. B. Jardine had become active in social welfare work. She founded the Omaha City Mission, located at first on North Tenth Street; it held religious services as well as assisting the poor. Director Nellie Magee moved the mission to a larger location on Pacific Street and broadened its activities.[2] Protestant women also dominated local temperance activities.

When the poor were essentially invisible, women journalists such as Elia Peattie publicized their living conditions. Beginning in 1888, her *Omaha World-Herald* column, A Word with the Women, portrayed low-income neighborhoods and paid tribute to women who helped them.

For example, Peattie described the "unwholesome scents" she found in Polish Sheelytown, at Twenty-Fourth and Vinton Streets. She noted the debris in the yards indicating "slovenly living," saloons, and a "rotten and miserable" tenement house called the "Beehive," with "half naked children" pouring from it.[3] However, in another stockyards neighborhood she discovered that "the little homes . . . are rather surprisingly comfortable." Children were playing outdoors or going to a schoolhouse on the hill. The people earned enough to buy homes with "the exercise of a little self-denial—or perhaps a good deal of self-denial."[4]

On other neighborhood tours she described the squalid conditions of "squatters" living in shanties in the "Bottoms" (today's East Omaha). Many were widows with children who could not afford to pay rent on the $1.50 a day they made from doing washing.[5] Peattie noted that despite the efforts of charitable groups, "the poor are being driven from shanties in the name of science."[6]

Peattie painted sympathetic portraits of women helping the needy through organizations like the Creche, a day nursery for children of single mothers at Nineteenth and Harney Streets. It was founded by Mrs. Thomas L. Kimball, mother of architect Thomas R. Kimball. Peattie saluted the matron, Mrs. Smith (no first name): "She knows just how much it will take to feed those hungry mouths: she has an idea of what to do for every sort of ailment. She can oversee the cooking in the way to make it at once most frugal and most tempting. There is a cook and two nurses and these comprise the entire working force. And it certainly takes that many women to comfortably look after such a family."[7]

Peattie also championed the YWCA because it provided inexpensive room and board for single working women at a house at Seventeenth Street and Dodge. On a visit she discovered that residents earned five or six dollars a week as stenographers, dressmakers, and phone operators. In her column she wrote: "When your income is a certain sum it happens that you have to make your own dresses after you have done your other work. Some of them went with generously disposed young men to see Amy Lelie coquet in rags and French silk stockings through 'La Mascotte.'"[8]

Worried about the YWCA's finances, Peattie suggested that "we could afford to lose a church or two. We cannot afford to lose the Working Girls boarding house."[9] In 1909 the YWCA moved to Seventeenth and St. Mary's. The new building lacked sleeping quarters but offered women a gym, basketball court, swimming pool, meeting rooms, and an auditorium, where feminists and suffragists could assemble.[10]

Other charities and advocacy groups founded before the turn

of the century included the YMCA in 1865, the Women's Christian Temperance Union in 1879, the Nebraska Children's Home Society in 1891, Lutheran Family Services in 1892, the Home of the Good Shepherd (for unwed mothers) in 1894, and the Visiting Nurses Association in 1896.

The Social Settlement Movement

At the turn of the last century Omaha women founded settlement houses modeled on Jane Addams's Hull House in Chicago. These neighborhood centers became community hubs that provided educational, health, cultural, and recreational services in addition to advocating for city services. They thrived throughout much of the twentieth century, but many of them closed in the early 2000s due to changing neighborhood conditions such as gentrification. Omaha's settlement houses included Social Settlement Association, which historically served white South Omahans, while Woodson Center served the area's African Americans. Wesley House served North Omaha, and Christ Child Society had its main center in "Little Italy," just south of downtown, with branches in North and South Omaha. Christ Child epitomized the role of settlement houses as neighborhood hubs and their partnerships with wealthy women volunteers.

Christ Child's Mary Flannigan

For forty years in the mid-twentieth century, Christ Child Society was almost synonymous with executive director Mary Flannigan, but the organization predated her by that long. It was founded in 1906 in a former mansion in the heart of Little Italy just south of downtown. Newspaper articles about the center's early days focus mostly on the fundraising efforts of rich female supporters.

Flannigan, a native of Stuart, Nebraska, joined Christ Child when she was a student at Creighton University. She moved into an apartment in the main center and lived at Christ Child for the rest of her life. After graduating from Creighton in 1946, she became the agency's second director, serving for forty-three years before retiring in 1986. During those years she became internationally recognized for her work in stabilizing her neighborhood and helping it adapt to change.[11] And everyone in the area knew this oversized, outgoing woman with a raucous laugh.

Spending a day with Flannigan (as I did as a reporter in the 1970s) illustrated settlement houses in action. Children from St. Frances Cabrini School played basketball in the gym, while senior citizens swam in the pool. Toddlers did art projects, and neighbors dropped by to socialize. The neighborhood association met there at night to solve problems with housing and traffic. Flannigan was involved in everything but especially enjoyed the children. When she retired, she estimated that she had worked with about forty thousand young people.

Flannigan served on the City Planning Board and the Mayor's Commission on Urban Renewal, was a delegate to the White House Conference on Youth, and was on an advisory committee for Omaha Public Schools. City officials credited her with helping the area adapt to the changes taking place.[12] She lived at Christ Child until she died in 2003. Her many honors included a prestigious medal from Pope John Paul II.[13]

Catholic Charities took over Christ Child in 2008 and closed the main center in 2015, due to declining enrollment in programs as the neighborhood changed.[14] But Christ Child still survives. Sue Seline, society president in 2019, said it has about one hundred members. Volunteers still assemble baby layettes for poor parents in a "pop-up fashion" at scattered locations. It also runs a scholarship program. "We do a lot of good without a lot of real estate," said Seline.[15]

In about the same era that settlement houses began, Father Edward Flanagan opened Boys Town to care for boys abandoned by destitute families. The female staff and volunteers were instrumental in running it. However, when Hollywood produced an Academy Award–winning movie on Boys Town, it ignored the contributions of these women.

The Women of Boys Town

After opening Boys Town in 1917, Flanagan battled just to survive to serve the growing numbers of abandoned boys; he got no church subsidy. The 1938 movie *Boys Town* shows cash pouring in to save the home when it was in danger. Viewers would never guess that Women's Bucket Brigade had collected money for Boys Town on every block in Omaha.

Mary Dolan Mullen, president of the Catholic Daughters of America, organized the effort to help rescue a faltering Flanagan fund drive. Women formed platoons that divided Omaha into sectors. Volunteers visited nearly every home and business (even speakeasies and pool halls) in their sectors, asking people to fill their buckets with cash. The Women's Bucket Brigade helped Flanagan raise the $200,000 needed to pay for Overlook Farm, the site of today's Boys Town.[16]

In reality Flanagan could never have run Boys Town without such female volunteers, to say nothing of the nuns who provided much of the daily care, said Boys Town historian Thomas Lynch.[17] Omaha philanthropist Catherine Nash gave Flanagan his first large donation of $10,000, and hosted the first meeting of the board of directors at her home.[18]

Boys Town traces its roots to the hotel for homeless men that Flanagan ran when he was a young priest.[19] After discovering how many abandoned boys there were, he received the bishop's permission to start a home for them. Although the church provided no funding, the bishop assigned three Notre Dame sisters to care for the boys.

In the *Boys Town* movie only Flanagan welcomes the first five boys to their new home in a downtown boardinghouse, leaving out the Notre Dames there who also greeted them.[20] The sisters cooked, kept house, and cared for the boys as the home moved first to the German-American House in South Omaha in 1918, then to its permanent location on Overlook Farm, ten miles west of Omaha, in 1921.

"They were the boys' mothers," said Lynch. "The boys loved them."[21] In addition to the Notre Dames, Omaha's Sisters of Mercy and German Franciscans from Missouri also helped staff Boys Town. In the 1940s the Franciscans assigned thirty to forty sisters to the home, where they handled everything from running the office to teaching in the campus school. The sisters earned only twenty-five cents a month, of which they were allowed to keep a nickel. Frequently, they used their token pay to treat the boys to sodas—a kindness that boys repaid by visiting the sisters in retirement in Chicago.[22]

Flanagan also relied heavily on women volunteers and fundraisers, including his relatives. During the Depression, before the movie made Boys Town famous, Flanagan published desperate appeals to keep Boys Town open. The women of America responded.

At sewing bees around the country, they collected nickels and dimes and sent them to Father Flanagan to feed his two hundred abandoned boys.[23] His mother, Honora of Omaha, started the Mothers Guild, which met weekly to sew quilts for the boys and to mend their clothing. Eventually, the Mothers Guild expanded, with a dozen chapters nationwide helping support the home.[24] All four of Flanagan's sisters also volunteered for or worked at Boys Town, including Theresa Mullen, who became postmistress when Boys Town acquired its own post office.[25]

Flanagan delivered speeches around the country that gained national press coverage after the movie had made Boys Town famous, and its financial woes became history. Flanagan died of a heart attack in Berlin in 1948 while on a mission for the War

Department to report on conditions for war orphans. He has been nominated for Roman Catholic sainthood.[26]

Boys Town itself grew so rich that the *Omaha Sun Newspapers* won a Pulitzer Prize for disclosing its wealth.[27] In response, Boys Town created family care homes on campus, opened programs in other cities, and sponsored specialized health research. Boys Town accepted its first five girls in 1978.[28] Now they are an integral part of Omaha's most famous human services institution. And women continue to play important roles of all types.

Boys Town exemplifies Omaha social services in the post–World War II era in one important respect: programs favored men and boys over girls and women. But that changed with the coming of the women's movement.

Background of a Revolution

During the 1950s and early 1960s Omaha added new human service facilities, notably its outstanding North and South Omaha Boys Clubs, which were designed to help combat juvenile delinquency. But the well-funded centers—with gyms, swimming pools, and game and craft rooms—that Mayor A. V. Sorensen promoted did not admit girls because they seemed to cause fewer problems than boys and therefore had less need for such facilities. The national Boys Club organization also excluded girls, so Omaha was not unusual. However, as local women awakened to racial and gender discrimination, activists, including some of Omaha's most prominent women, were determined to end such discrimination.

Fighting Inequality

In the late 1960s, when Susan Buffett, late wife of legendary financier Warren Buffett, quit the Junior League of Omaha in protest over its failure to fund the early education program Head Start, the move signaled that change was coming, said Barbara Haggart, a prominent Junior League of Omaha leader and human services activist.[29]

Both African American and white women pushed to expand day care, create equal facilities for boys and girls, and help victims of sexual assault and domestic violence. They began demanding a voice in making human services decisions, especially those related to funding. "Women found their voice. They started recognizing their power and acting on it," said Mclarney. "In effect they said, 'if we don't do this, who will and nothing would change.'"[30]

Change involved some nasty conflicts. In 1973, for example, the YWCA fired its entire staff and dropped out of United Way. United Way had demanded that the YWCA modernize its programs and serve more people, which it eventually did, before rejoining United Way.

Under the leadership of Emily Cunningham Kozlik, the YWCA started serving victims of sexual assault and opened programs to help low-income women find employment, such as a program that provides free interview and work attire. Today the YWCA has become the Women's Center for Advancement, after dropping its national affiliation.

United Way became a focal point of women's demands for more decision-making power and greater funding for services for women and girls, Haggart said. "With the ERA [proposed Equal Rights Amendment] movement coming, women's and girls' issues bubbled up. They were hard to ignore," said Haggart, the first woman to chair a United Way budget panel, where funding recommendations were developed.[31] The "young Turks" like Haggart demanded that United Way help open a Girls Club remotely comparable to the North and South Omaha Boys Clubs.

"Boys did disruptive, violent things so it was important to get them off the streets. Girls didn't do those things so people didn't worry about them so much," said Haggart.[32] The advocates for girls (among them some men) faced stiff opposition.

The Boys Club saw no need for a Girls Club, said Mclarney. "The Boys Club thought they should get the money and figure it out."[33] However, newly assertive women on the United Way board and budget panels, backed by groups like the Junior League of Omaha, won. The Girls Club of Omaha opened in 1975 in a North Omaha church basement, a far cry from the facilities for boys.

Under the leadership of executive director Mary Heng-Braun, it moved from that basement to its own building, expanded into South Omaha, and created nationally recognized innovative programs such as one that taught girls how to protect themselves from assault. Heng-Braun later became director of the Women's Fund of Omaha.

Haggart, who led the fight for a large Junior League project for the Girls Club, said the battle energized Omaha's wealthy and influential female "career volunteers," who were well educated and knew how to get things done. The Young Turks encouraged them "to take things further and probably gave them more clout," said Haggart.[34]

"These women were professional volunteers," said Mclarney. "They weren't confrontational, but they put their money where their mouths were." They got the funding required to create a Girls Club.[35] The Girls Club of Omaha became Girls Incorporated (now called Girls Inc.) after the Boys Club admitted girls and changed its name to the Boys and Girls Club. Girls Inc.'s top supporters, Warren Buffett and his daughter, Susan, helped ensure its future. In additions, Susan Buffett's Sherwood Foundation is a major donor to many programs fighting poverty.

Wealthy women also fought for a shelter for domestic violence victims, which Catholic Social Services (today's Catholic Charities) opened in the late 1970s. (A personal note: I covered this battle and will never forget that the shelter filled immediately and had a waiting list before noon of its first day. The head of Catholic Social Services was distraught to discover the large need and immediately began planning a second shelter. I also learned that some wealthy women had made their donations contingent on United Way starting the shelter.)

United Way has also changed since the 1970s, when a study showed that women were 80 percent of United Way agency volunteers but held only 30 percent of the seats on governing boards.[36] In the 1980s and 1990s its presidents included prominent women such as Sharon Marvin and Kate Dodge, and it hired women for top staff positions.

Grassroots Advocacy: LaFern Williams

African American women also began demanding attention to their problems, such as a lack of day care services in low-income neighborhoods. LaFern Williams, a single mother from South Omaha, led the movement.

Williams worked tirelessly to improve life for poor women and children. Although the vast majority of Omaha's Black residents lived in North Omaha, several thousand lived in South Omaha, many in South Side Terrace Homes, where Williams raised her family. In 1968 she helped organize a welfare rights group and lobbied the Nebraska Legislature for increased welfare benefits. She also testified at a congressional hearing on human rights.[37] Williams and her group, Mothers for Self Help, sought to get mothers out of poverty by providing them with the day care services that would allow them to get job training. They persuaded the Omaha Housing Authority to rent them an apartment for a Kiddie Kollege childcare center. It was limited to just twelve children, but it was a start.

As part of her organizing efforts, Williams served on numerous boards and South Omaha community improvement groups. In 1978, three years after Williams's death, a large new day care center named for her opened at Thirty-Third and Q Streets.[38]

A Volunteer Leader: Marian Andersen

During this era the prominent "professional volunteers" who devoted their lives to unpaid community service scored their own "firsts," comparable to those of women in business and politics. Marian Andersen, widow of *Omaha World-Herald* publisher Harold Andersen, exemplifies the power and authority that women such as Margre Durham, Mary Landen, Gail Koch, Dr. Gail Yanney, and others began to exercise during the 1970s and 1980s.

Andersen, a Lincoln native who graduated Phi Beta Kappa from the University of Nebraska, reflected on her years of opening volunteer leadership doors for women locally and nationally: "The difference between a volunteer and a professional is that a professional plans her vacation around her work while a volunteer plans her work around her vacation."[39] Among other roles she served as vice chair of the national Red Cross Board and president of the Heartland Chapter of the American Red Cross; first woman chair of the University of Nebraska Foundation; and member of the national Public Broadcasting System Board.

Andersen said that she never joined a board "unless I could make a difference," and she nearly always held leadership positions because being a leader came naturally to her. "Some men were surprised that I could command a room with all men," she said. "Speaking ability is important. I don't mind speaking extemporaneously." Dedication to causes and a sense of civic responsibility also are important. "You have to do something."[40]

Among other accomplishments, Andersen co-founded both the Nebraska Shakespeare Festival and the Tocqueville Society, consisting of major donors to United Way. She was president of the Junior League of Omaha and a member of numerous major boards, such as Planned Parenthood, Joslyn Art Museum, and the Omaha Community Playhouse. She endowed the Nebraska Women Journalists Hall of Fame that is named in her honor and has received numerous awards.[41]

Women in Today's Human Services

The era of professional volunteers who devoted their lives to full-time community service is passing, according to Barbara Haggart, who turned her volunteer experience into a job at the Greater Omaha Chamber of Commerce, screening nonprofit funding requests to corporations. She explained that young women who came of age during the women's movement usually volunteered while holding full-time jobs, just as men have done. A great many continued working and volunteering while raising their families rather than quit their jobs for a few years.[42]

Michael Mclarney said that the community benefits from women integrating careers with volunteerism. "United Way is a community table, and we need people of all kinds at the table. We focused on bringing in women who were thought leaders in the community."[43]

Women have led the fight for new services. For example, Connie Spellman, retired head of Omaha by Design, advocated for early childhood education; the College of Saint Mary named its early childhood education center for her. Project Harmony battles sex trafficking, and agencies like the Salvation Army long ago closed outmoded services such as a maternity hospital for unwed mothers. But some things haven't changed since the days of Mary Lucretia Creighton. Women remain in the forefront of human services work in Omaha.

8

Culture and the Arts

Omaha was slow to develop local cultural life. Residents could attend performances by traveling theatrical troops, occasional concerts and music festivals, vaudeville shows, and bicycle races. However, the Trans-Mississippi and International Exposition awakened Omaha to the economic importance of the arts. After it ended, Sarah Joslyn became the patroness of the arts in Omaha and personally paid for its most important museum. Later generations of women continued to make major contributions to culture in Omaha.

The Trans-Mississippi, however, was the turning point for the arts in Omaha, and before it even opened, planners treated the city to a lively battle over how women should be depicted.

Trans-Mississippi Exposition's Art Battles

In 1898 beauty contests were associated with circuses and freak shows, not major events like the Trans-Mississippi Exposition. So, when male officials announced a competition for young women's faces to appear on the fair medallion, Omaha's upper-class women involved in running the exposition were horrified. Yes, horrified! Weren't *they* supposed to be in charge of cultural events? The men considered the medallion competition a harmless publicity stunt, but the women were insulted. The controversy raged in local papers before the promoters won.

Young women in twenty-two states submitted their photos to newspapers to identify the ideal features of the medal's face.[1] To ensure that contestants were respectable, regional women's boards vouched for the entrants' moral character.[2] But the battle continued.

Fair officials decided to sell the photos to help support the Girls and Boys Building over the objections of Education Board secretary Frances Ford, who stated: "We have not been asked to take these photographs and exhibit and we object most decidedly to the announcement being made that we will do so. We do not want them and will not exhibit them under any circumstances." Nonetheless, local newspapers carried the photos with contestants' names and information about their achievements, hobbies, and family backgrounds.[3]

Later two Salvation Army officers got so upset with a sculpture of a voluptuous kneeling nude women that they attacked it. They climbed the Arch of the States at the Twentieth Street entrance and hacked off an arm and a leg.[4]

The Trans-Mississippi made the arts an issue in a community that was six years old before it had its first theatrical performance.

The Arts in Early Omaha

Omaha got a slow start in the arts.[5] The city's first theatrical event, a play featuring Julia Dean Hayne, was held at the Herndon House in 1860, six years after the city's birth.[6] Seven years later Omaha's first theater, the Academy of Music, opened.[7] Boyd's Opera House followed in 1881 with a seating capacity of seventeen hundred, expanding the city's capacity for music and theatrical events.[8] Boyd later built a second theater.

While Sorensen's *Story of Omaha* includes a chapter on "Early Amusements," describing such events as the British Blondes theater troupe's visit to Omaha in the late 1880s, a collection of Elia Peattie's columns on women in the *Omaha World-Herald* in that period includes nothing on the arts. Sorenson highlights the British Blondes because one member remained in Omaha for a year and dated a local man before returning to London to perform in the Theatre Royal.[9]

In 1888 George W. Lininger, a wealthy farm implements dealer and art patron, opened a gallery connected to his home to display his collection, the closest thing to a museum in Omaha. It was open to the public on a limited basis under the auspices of the Western Art Association, but the gallery closed after Lininger's death in 1907.[10]

In 1856 the Omaha Public Library Association opened the first public library, but the association folded after three years. In 1871 the city's second Library Association opened in rented quarters at Fourteenth and Dodge Streets. Because subscriptions and lecture ticket sales did not earn enough to support the association, in 1877 the tax-supported Omaha Public Library took over its collection and facilities.[11] Most of the early librarians were women, just as they are today. Edith Tobitt, library director from 1898 to 1934, turned the library into Omaha's de facto art museum by hosting art exhibits on the third floor.[12]

Women-Run Culture at the Trans-Mississippi

Cultural activities were an important component of world fairs in the 1890s, which meant that Omaha's exposition also had to feature music, the graphic arts, and artistic events. Upper-class women ran the Trans-Mississippi's committees on education and entertainment. The Board of Education managed the Girls and Boys Building, all educational features of the exposition, and all branches of women's work.[13] They also ran the Ladies Bureau of Entertainment, which hosted important visitors.[14] They wanted to persuade two million visitors that Omaha had a lively cultural environment.

A number of rising professional women who had art studios in the Paxton Block, where the exposition was headquartered, did graphic and exhibit design work and helped organize the grounds into "zoned" neighborhoods. These allowed respectable upper-class women to move about freely and to safely enjoy the fair.[15]

Unlike the separate women's buildings at previous international expositions elsewhere, the Trans-Mississippi featured an Education Building housing art displays and events that appealed to both women and men. It sponsored the Arts Congress, which showcased regional culture, such as Omaha Indians performing their tribal music.[16] The Liberal Arts Building displayed the work of both male and female artists. Women lectured on the arts, and club women staffed exhibitions on western topics such as how to cook with corn. Blue-collar women staffed ostrich farms, perfume counters, and restaurants as well as performing along the Midway.[17]

The Bureau of Entertainment presented Omaha as a refined place to live at elaborate social events held for important visitors. For example, it organized a luncheon at the Omaha Club honoring Mrs. William McKinley when she and President McKinley visited the exposition. Although the first lady could not attend due to illness, the wives of cabinet officers and diplomatic corps who accompanied the president were impressed. One participant called it "the most elaborate and one of the most brilliant entertainments of the summer."

The Entertainment Bureau also organized an elaborate Flower Parade and a masked carnival held on the pavement of the Court of Honor flanking the lagoon that ran through the exposition.[18] Sarah Joslyn, an avid gardener and orchid collector whose husband, George Joslyn, was one of Omaha's wealthiest men, was a prominent member of the bureau. After the exposition, Sarah worked for the arts until she died.

Sarah Joslyn and the Arts

Sarah Joslyn, a native of Vermont, was the founding mother of the arts in Omaha. She came to Omaha with her husband, George, in 1879 or 1880, when he opened a branch office of Iowa Printing called the Omaha Newspaper Union. It produced printing equipment, stock typefaces, newsprint, and electroplate and stereotype plate copy for local newspapers. Eventually, he built the Western Newspaper Union into an empire that monopolized the nation's auxiliary printing industry. In the process he became a multimillionaire and Omaha's wealthiest resident.[19]

Although Sarah received only a grade school education, she was an avid reader. Penelope Smith, who set up the archives for the Joslyn Castle Board, described her as "practical" and dedicated to doing things that she thought "were her moral and social responsibility." "She was never part of the in crowd here. She had money but not a lot of patience for people who put on airs. When she gave a party, it was to bring people together to achieve a goal," usually to raise money for a worthy cause.[20]

The Joslyn home, originally called Lynhurst, is a work of art in itself. This spectacular thirty-five-room Scottish baronial castle at 3902 Davenport Street is today called Joslyn Castle and has become a museum that is listed on the National Register of Historic Places as well as Omaha's Landmarks.[21] It features stained glass windows, fine woodwork, and a large music room for recitals.

The Joslyns also built a carriage house for their collection of automobiles and a greenhouse for Sarah's flowers. The 1913 Easter Sunday tornado destroyed the greenhouse and heavily damaged other nearby buildings, including St. Barnabas Episcopal Church. Although the Joslyns were Unitarians, Sarah helped fund St. Barnabas's repairs.[22]

This was typical of the couple's philanthropy. Both Sarah and George gave generously to charities, including Omaha University, the Nebraska Humane Society, the Unitarian Church, Child Saving Institution, and the Old People's Home.[23] Sarah also was a national officer of the Humane Society.

After working on the Trans-Mississippi Exposition, she volunteered at art exhibits at the public library, which heightened her awareness of Omaha's need for a museum. In 1914 she worked on a Fine Arts Society drive to raise $50,000 to buy the Turner Mansion at 3316 Farnam Street and convert it into a museum. The society abandoned the project after raising $30,000 and returned the money, saying it could not raise the rest. However, disagreements over the location might have been the real problem.

Efforts to start a museum halted during World War I but resumed in 1920.[24] Museum advocates proposed a bond issue for a new library that would include an art museum, but the idea failed due to lack of enthusiasm for replacing the library.

Mrs. Ward Burgess, president of the Fine Arts Society, paid for Maurice Block, a former curator of the Chicago Art Institute, to become the society's director and build a museum.[25] Block organized lectures and exhibits at the library but antagonized some Omahans by criticizing the West for neglecting the arts.[26]

In 1922 Sarah took control. She announced that she would build a museum on land she had purchased at Twenty-Fourth and Dodge Streets as a memorial to George, who had died in 1916. She would finance it with the fortune she and George had accumulated.[27] "Sarah was always an equal partner with George, and he trusted her totally to handle his estate," said Smith.

Joslyn told the *Omaha Daily News*: "I do think the Omaha Society of Fine Arts deserves a home of its own. Each Sunday during the past month, I have been acting as hostess at the art galleries in the city library; and I was surprised at the public interest in the exhibits."[28] She hired noted local architects John and Alan McDonald to design the building.[29]

After six years of research, Joslyn held another press conference to announce her gift of $3 million (equivalent to $43 million today) for construction and specific plans for the museum. The *World-Herald*'s May 6, 1928, front page proclaimed the news in a banner headline, "Mrs. Joslyn to Build Memorial," along with an artist's sketch of the proposed building. It would be a magnificent marble art deco structure with columns at the main entrance on the east side.[30] A *World-Herald* editorial reflected on the importance of the museum to Omaha's future: "The Joslyn memorial will give a tremendous impetus to cultural activity in Omaha where magnificent strides have been made in the past few years. If Omaha can keep its pioneer zest for doing things, retain its vigorous interest in material achievement, and come also to a sympathetic understanding of the highest expression of civilization, it will always be a tolerant, liberal happy community in which to have a home."[31]

Joslyn sold her majority ownership in the family firm to fund the museum and eventually spent more than $4 million (more than $50 million today) building it.[32] The Joslyn Museum opened on November 29, 1931, and in 1938 it was listed as one of the one hundred best buildings in the United States.[33] In addition to a concert hall, it included an airy marble fountain court and galleries. The *World-Herald* estimated that about twenty-five thousand people visited on the first day alone.[34] Opening-day activities included a concert performed on the organ, which had been moved from Joslyn Castle.

Joslyn, who died in 1940, also helped found the Omaha Community Playhouse (OCP) in 1924, the same year that the Omaha Symphony was established. The Playhouse's first president was the architect Alan McDonald.[35]

Dodie Brando, mother of actor Marlon Brando, starred in the OCP's first play, *The Enchanted Cottage*, at the Mary Cooper Dance Studio in 1925. The cast also included Henry Fonda's sister Jayne, and he debuted there in *You and I* six months later.[36]

However, the Playhouse needed its own theater. In 1928 Joslyn donated pastureland at Fortieth and Davenport Streets as the site of a "temporary" theater. It housed the Playhouse until it moved to Sixty-Ninth and Cass in 1959.

Enter the Junior League

Volunteerism of all kinds in Omaha got a boost when three wealthy young women organized the Junior League of Omaha (JLO) in 1919. However, arts groups especially benefited from the organization, which taught young society women how to organize and raise money. League projects included working with the Omaha Children's Theater and starting guilds to support Joslyn Museum and the symphony. Jeanne Salerno, league president in 1979–80, said cultural projects were especially popular "because they seemed like more fun."[37]

In 1933 the league began sponsoring the Omaha Children's Theater, and members annually produced and performed in a play to benefit it.[38] Among those assigned to the Children's Theater was Mary Elizabeth "Emmy" Jonas Gifford, a New York–trained artist and JLO co-founder, who became one of Omaha's most important cultural leaders. Late in life she finally reclaimed her identity as a professional artist.

Emmy Gifford: Children's Theater, Artist, and Philanthropist

When Emmy Jonas moved from Omaha to New York City to launch her artistic career in 1932, she was armed with a fine arts degree from Smith College in Massachusetts and the financial backing of her father, a prominent Omaha doctor. She spent five years studying at the Art Students League, a prestigious national studio arts school.

Even so, she struggled to find a job as an artist, drawing cartoons for newspapers in Omaha and Chicago while she hunted. She tried unsuccessfully to persuade the editors of the *New Yorker* to accept her sketches and Macy's Department Store to accept her design proposals. In 1937 she returned to Omaha, where she married Dr. Hal Gifford, an ophthalmologist.[39]

Despite her professional arts training, "there was no place [in Omaha] for women artists at the time," said Gifford's son Charles, an Omaha architect. "Her life was a reaction to being considered an amateur."[40] Instead, she became a combination of artist, volunteer, fundraiser, and philanthropist in the Omaha arts world.

"Because she was a dutiful daughter, she did come back here but she said in effect that you made me come back here, but I'll do it my way," said Audrey Kauders, a retired Joslyn Museum executive and former director of the Museum of Nebraska Art in Kearney. "If she couldn't be a working artist in Omaha, she found other ways to use her skill and her compulsion to do art."[41]

Gifford's primary artistic outlet became the Omaha Children's Theater, which was renamed the Emmy Gifford Children's Theater in 1977. Her lifelong friend, former Omahan and Academy Award winner Henry Fonda, attended the tribute dinner in 1978. (In 1986 the organization moved from the old Center Theater to the renovated Astro Theater and changed its name to the Rose Blumkin Performing Arts Center in honor of Rose Blumkin of the Nebraska Furniture Mart, who funded the renovation.)

Ironically, said Charles Gifford, his mother was "not terribly fond of children. She got involved in junior theater as an end run around the problem of being a woman artist in Omaha."[42]

Gifford wrote or rewrote some plays while designing sets and costumes for more than five hundred productions. She represented Omaha at national and international junior theater conferences and won awards from such groups. She also appeared in a number of Omaha Community Playhouse productions before the theater discovered her talent for producing costumes and sets in addition to fundraising. In 1973 she received the Playhouse's highest award for her forty-two years of service.[43]

Gifford also created plywood mannequins for a Nebraska Centennial display of historic costumes at Joslyn in 1967 and made documentary films for Children's Hospital, the Visiting Nurse Association, and the YWCA.[44] However, Gifford always self-identified as an artist, said Charles. "She worked on her art every day" in her studio in the Giffords' Tudor home at Thirty-Sixth and Burt since she hired others to cook, clean, and shop.

Charles, the youngest of her four children (one of whom died young), said he "enjoyed benign neglect" from his mother when he was growing up, and he was raised mostly as an only child because his siblings were older.[45] His sister Jessie became a well-known artist in New York. Gifford worked in drawing, oil, watercolor, silk screen, polyester resin, costumes, set design, illustration, cartoon, and poster design.[46] The women's movement finally freed her to claim her identity as a professional artist.[47]

Kauders described Emmy Gifford's style as "realist" because "she was a little early for abstraction. She was a keen observer of people and did a lot of drawings and sketches of people. Their personalities come across." One of her best works was a self-portrait that Charles donated to MONA.[48]

In 1979 Gifford began marketing her work, selling some pieces at an invitation-only event at her home. She began signing her pieces as "Emmy Gifford," instead of M. E. Gifford or M. E. Jonas, and in the 1980s she joined the Artists' Co-op Gallery in the Old Market.

In 1982 she held another "by invitation" exhibition at her home featuring forty sculptures, including dragons, mythical characters, and masks she had produced for theater productions. Her semi-abstract sculptures made her a recognized contemporary artist.[49]

Gifford and her husband, Hal, also remained pillars of Omaha society, with Hal becoming King of Aksarben for his work with Fontenelle Forest. Emmy died in 1997, at the age of eighty-seven.

In 2004 the Museum of Nebraska Art held a retrospective of Emmy's work.[50] "We can be thankful that she lived long enough to have the satisfaction of assuming her identity," said Kauders.[51]

Gifford, however, never had to support herself with her art, as did Ree Schonlau Kaneko, a founder of contemporary arts in Omaha.

Ree Schonlau Kaneko

By the time Ree Schonlau began her art career, in the 1960s, the modern local arts scene was taking shape in the Old Market. The area just south of downtown had morphed from a fruit and vegetable market to an infant arts haven, where old warehouses could be converted into studios. Upscale businesses including galleries, bars, coffeehouses, and gourmet restaurants began opening. Street festivals and art fairs found a home in the Old Market and downtown. Musicians entertained on street corners. Creative young people began moving in. At last Omaha had a neighborhood centered around the arts.

A key figure in this transformation was Ree Schonlau, who founded the Bemis Center for Contemporary Arts, originally called the Alternative Worksite, in 1981. Later she and her husband, acclaimed sculptor Jun Kaneko, founded KANEKO, a gallery and creative program.

Schonlau grew up in the Little Italy area of Omaha and received a BFA degree in ceramics from Omaha University in 1968. She moved to New York to explore artistic opportunities but returned to Omaha in 1971. She worked as a studio artist and founded the Ree Schonlau Gallery as well as the Craftsman's Guild and Omaha Brickworks, all in the Old Market.[52]

By 1981, when Schonlau, her future husband, and two others founded the Alternative Worksite, the Old Market was the home of the Artists' Cooperative Gallery, which featured the work of many women artists. Originally, the Alternative Worksite placed artists in industrial settings, but eventually, under Schonlau's leadership, it became internationally recognized for its artist-in-residence and exhibition program. Artists from all over the world compete to come to Omaha to work in the free studio spaces in the converted Bemis Bag Center at Twelfth and Leavenworth Streets. The Bemis Center also displays their works and does other cultural programming.[53] Some of these artists, such as Creighton University sculpture professor Littleton Alston, stayed, strengthening the Omaha arts community.

In 1998 Schonlau and Kaneko founded KANEKO, a "complex of creativity spaces" that features a large gallery of contemporary art housed in a converted warehouse near the Bemis Center. Now it is a significant tourist attraction.

In 2012, when Ree and Jun Kaneko were inducted into the Omaha Business Hall of Fame for building the Omaha arts community, she praised the patrons who had supported their avant-garde efforts. "Any mature city's going to have the arts involved in it. . . . The cultural in-fill has finally caught up with those of us who were out here hanging on."[54]

It is interesting to note that Schonlau's work gained the strong support and financial backing of local business leaders, especially members of the Simon family, who owned Omaha Steaks. They realized that the arts helped Omaha attract high-tech entrepreneurs and other businesses offering the jobs of the future.

Omaha Women and Culture

Today more women like Ree Schonlau Kaneko are playing important roles in Omaha's arts community. However, still more women work as fundraisers, donors, and volunteers than as artists, said Kauders, a former deputy director of Joslyn.

Women artists like Gifford have struggled to be taken seriously, especially if they were wealthy and did not need to make money from their work, she said. Often such women have been considered hobbyists and have had to find outlets for their gifts because it was not acceptable to be an artist. Usually, artists of both genders have held other jobs, such as teaching, to support themselves while doing art or theater part-time.[55]

From World War I to World War II

In 1919, when the Nebraska Legislature finally ratified the Nineteenth Amendment, women unlocked not only the ballot box but many other opportunities. During the 1920s Omaha women cut their hair, shortened their skirts, gained new roles in business, and expanded their involvement in arts and human services. Women were on the move.

But some things did not change. Vice continued to thrive, and Prohibition had no impact on reducing drinking as temperance activists had hoped. Racial hostilities increased, culminating in the infamous courthouse riot of 1919.[1]

The Courthouse Riot of 1919

During World War I Omaha's Black population doubled, growing to over ten thousand by 1920, part of the national exodus of African Americans from the South. Many of Omaha's new African American residents found jobs in the packinghouses, but there were no Black teachers or public officials. The influx created social pressures that led to the courthouse riot of September 1919, which killed William Brown, a Black prisoner falsely accused of assaulting a white woman, and severely wounded Mayor Edward Smith.[2]

The horror began when a crowd gathered as Brown was jailed

at the courthouse on September 26. Two days later several hundred South Omaha high school boys marched to the courthouse to "get the N——." When older and more violent men joined the crowd, rioting broke out, complete with shooting and the throwing of firebombs through the courthouse's windows. After Mayor Edward Smith arrived to try to control the crowd, which had grown to five thousand, the crowd demanded that police hand Brown over to them. Rioters stormed the building and assaulted Smith.

Police had taken Brown and other prisoners to the roof for safekeeping, but other prisoners threw Brown down a staircase into the hands of the mob. He was beaten, shot, stripped, and castrated before his body was tied to an auto and dragged through the streets. Then the crowd burned his dead body. Smith was badly injured, and a white boy was killed by a stray bullet.[3]

The riot attracted horrified national attention, and the *Omaha World-Herald* received a Pulitzer Prize for its editorial attacking "jungle rule" and the "mob spirit" of the "wolf pack."[4] Omaha has never fully erased its reputation for racism.

The Prohibition Era in a Wide-Open City

In 1917 Nebraska went dry, two years before the nation, but Omahans continued drinking, and vice continued to openly flourish. Gambling was legal, prostitution was illegal but largely ignored, and in 1929, a dozen years after Prohibition began, Omaha had fifteen hundred drinking establishments.[5] Political boss Tom Dennison protected the city's three breweries and one distillery, keeping them open.[6] A number of Omaha's best modern restaurants began as speakeasies during this period, and many Omahans also made home-brewed beer and bathtub gin.

Omaha was noted for its colorful crime. Bess Furman, a White House correspondent who had been a reporter in Omaha during the 1920s, delighted in Little Italy, where "a murder for the honor of a woman marked many a Saturday night" and where criminals were often interesting characters who made good newspaper copy.[7] Nebraska abandoned Prohibition more than a year after it ended nationally in 1933.[8] During Prohibition some women joined their husbands in bootlegging, but after it ended, a number of them opened popular Italian restaurants.

Women on the Move

The post–World War I era opened new opportunities to Omaha women. In 1922 the Omaha Chamber of Commerce established its Women's Division, an outgrowth of the Omaha Business and Professional Women League. This gave women their first voice in this key organization.[9] Women, especially Sarah Joslyn, boosted local cultural expansion. Her much-anticipated Joslyn Art Museum opened in 1931, and its concert hall opened a year later.[10]

Newspapers covered the changing lives and roles of women, with stories on women telephone operators, women doctors, and women's organizations discussing social and economic policy. In a random sampling of 1926 *Omaha World-Herald*s, articles mention women's careers in engagement announcements, and one society page story featured an Aksarben duchess practicing shooting.[11]

The Depression and World War II

The 1929 stock market crash ushered in the Great Depression. In Nebraska extreme drought and nightmarish dust storms added to the misery of massive unemployment. The state's population declined, although Omaha's population grew from about 190,000 in 1920 to almost 224,000 in 1940, absorbing those who had abandoned their farms during the Depression. The New Deal provided public works jobs that saved Omaha from economic catastrophe. Manufacturing jobs declined, but federal programs employed residents in improving streets, parks, and sewers and in building housing projects, public buildings, and the South Omaha bridge.[12]

Women lost jobs faster than men as employers fired "secondary wage earners" to keep married men employed. Married teachers often lost their jobs, and women sometimes either stayed single or married secretly in order to keep their jobs. Eventually, women regained their jobs faster than men because they usually worked in traditional female fields like clerical work, nursing, and domestic service, which came back faster than manufacturing.[13]

During World War II Omaha women temporarily replaced men in many jobs, including running the city's streetcars. Thousands of local Rosie the Riveters built planes at the Glenn Martin Bomber Plant located at today's Offutt Air Force Base.[14] However, when the war ended, many women lost their jobs to men returning from the armed services. They either took traditional women's jobs or returned to homemaking and raising the Baby Boom generation in a city poised for postwar growth.

9

Business

Long before the women's movement brought large numbers of women into nontraditional business jobs, women joined their husbands in running family businesses or started their own companies. These were usually neighborhood grocery stores or restaurants, but some grew into major companies like Mutual of Omaha and the Nebraska Furniture Mart.

Big corporations hired thousands of women as clerical workers and phone operators, confining them to the "pink-collar" ghetto. Even after the women's movement, only a handful of women broke the glass ceiling into top jobs. Many women complained that Omaha businesses treated women worse than employers in other cities. The women's movement brought mentoring programs to help women become business and community leaders.

Women of the Omaha Business Hall of Fame

Omaha's first successful businesswoman, Anna Wilson, isn't in the Omaha Business Hall of Fame, but that's what happens when you make your fortune in the world's oldest profession. Wilson left her $1 million ($29 million today) fortune from investing in downtown real estate to charity, but she's still waiting for the Greater Omaha Chamber of Commerce to formally recognize her achievements.

Only a small percentage of the Hall of Fame's members are women, including such obvious choices as Mabel Criss of Mutual and United of Omaha, "Mrs. B" of the Nebraska Furniture Mart, Janice Stoney of U.S. West, and *Omaha Star* publisher Mildred Brown. Other inductees have played important roles in their family businesses, started successful businesses, and led major institutions.[1] Ironically, Marian Ivers, late executive vice president of the chamber who started several important mentoring programs, had not been inducted as of 2021.

Women in Family Businesses

Although the "moms" were as important as the "pops" in running Omaha family businesses, they tended to work behind the scenes, keeping the books or managing the office, while their husbands ran operations, said Lyn Wallin Ziegenbein, executive director emerita of the Peter Kiewit Foundation. If a man died young, his widow often ran the business until the next generation took over.

Women influenced their male relatives, some of whom became corporate titans.[2] Peter Kiewit, for example, credited his German immigrant mother, Anna, with giving him the drive and work ethic to turn their family bricklaying business into a world-class construction company. He and his wife, Evelyn, donated Kiewit Hall to Creighton University in her memory.[3]

"Women in business tended to hide their light under a bush," said Ziegenbein. "Unless someone else said let it shine, it wouldn't. The money a [family] business made was usually attributed to the men."[4] However, when a business failed, women like Ellen Swanson Ashford, of Nebraska Clothing, sometimes had to pick up the pieces. Her father had founded the high-end clothing store and chose her husband, Don, to manage it, even though she was always involved in the company.

Nebraska Clothing's Resilient Ellen Swanson Ashford

During the 1950s, when Nebraska Clothing was one of the nation's top clothing stores, Ellen Ashford worked with the most well-known names in the country's fashion industry, said her son, former U.S. representative Brad Ashford. She hosted Ralph Lauren at her home in Fairacres whenever he came to Omaha. If a customer needed a dress for a special occasion, Ashford would call Oscar de la Renta for help. She flew select customers to Los Angeles for exclusive showings that movie stars attended.[5]

Ellen's father, Otto Swanson, a Swedish immigrant, had built Nebraska Clothing into Omaha's largest high-end clothing store. He also was renowned for having co-founded Omaha's National Conference of Christians and Jews affiliate. The king of Sweden honored him for helping Jews persecuted by the Nazis. And when he retired, he turned the business over to Ellen's husband, Don, a war hero.

Ellen, however, was always a force in her own right at a time when few wealthy women had careers. Her Poppy Shop (a store within the store) sold designer clothing to affluent women. She combined merchandise buying trips to New York with attending meetings of the Junior League of America board, on which she was vice president. Eventually, she quit the board to spend more time raising her three sons.[6]

During the 1970s, when downtown stores like Nebraska Clothing lost business to suburban shopping centers, Don Ashford opened stores in malls that the company couldn't afford. He also developed mental and physical health problems that affected the business because "there's very little separation emotionally and economically in the day-to-day work of a family business. When you have a family-owned business, it's always about the family," said Brad Ashford. As a result of these factors, Nebraska Clothing failed.

Finally, Ellen and Don separated, and she became president of the firm. She had to manage its dissolution, although she wasn't responsible for its collapse.[7] Ellen, who never divorced her husband, sold stores to pay off creditors rather than declare bankruptcy. Retaining the Poppy Shop name, she opened her own fine clothing store at Seventy-Sixth and Pacific. She still sold dresses to her wealthy friends and outfitted the Aksarben coronation. Later she moved the store to Countryside Village. Meanwhile, her husband opened a small clothing store in the Old Market Passageway, but it failed.[8]

After Don's death, Ellen married John Anderson, who had formerly been married to Don's sister. She continued working at her store until 1991, just days before she died of ovarian cancer at age sixty-one. "She was the most resilient person I ever met except for my wife," said Brad Ashford.[9]

Doris Shukert: Co-running the Family Meat Business

Few Omaha family businesses were as glamorous as Nebraska Clothing, certainly not the meat business that Doris and Nathan Shukert operated in downtown Omaha. While Ellen Ashford was hobnobbing with celebrity designers, Doris Shukert ran the machines at Shukert's Meats when required, even though her title was business manager, according to her son, former Omaha city planning director Marty Shukert.[10] The business included both a wholesale operation and a separate kosher meat operation. Nathan focused on sales and marketing, while Doris kept the books and managed other operations. "My mother was the glue that kept the business going," said Marty Shukert. "Both worked long, hard hours, but she was the stabilizing influence. They made decisions together."

Nathan's father had previously run a kosher meat market at Twenty-Fourth and Decatur Streets when that was an immigrant Jewish neighborhood. Ethnic businesses such as groceries and bakeries often closed when the people they served moved elsewhere, as the Jewish community did.[11]

Shukert's Meats "was a typical mom-and-pop shop," Marty Shukert said. "The owners of the business and their family did everything." He recalled making hamburgers for local McDonald's stores at a time when they bought fresh local meat instead of frozen national beef. "There was no separation between family and business. You didn't leave work at the business, and there weren't a lot of hours to leave it there. My parents worked from 6:30 a.m. to 10:00 p.m."

Doris had been a homemaker when Marty and his brother, Jamie, were little, but she got heavily involved in the business when Marty was about thirteen and Jamie was eight. Doris would come home late in the afternoon to fix dinner but would return to work later if there was an equipment breakdown or a problem in the kosher portion of the business, which shipped Nathan's popular corned beef to customers nationally.[12]

Doris retired after the Shukerts sold their business in 1980, but she volunteered for Children's Hospital and Dodge Elementary School, which her grandchildren attended. She died in 2007.[13]

Women in Omaha Corporations

Only a handful of the women in the Omaha Business Hall of Fame worked for major corporations because very few have risen to their top ranks. A 2016 Women's Fund of Omaha study found that some 83 percent of local CEOs were men and that men held more than 80 percent of local corporate board seats. Women, however, were common in middle management.[14] But a few local women have broken the glass ceiling, sometimes because they owned the "building." Mabel Criss became a top executive at Mutual of Omaha after she and her husband bought a small insurance agency that they built into a national giant.

Building Mutual of Omaha: Mabel Criss

"The greatest woman executive in America." That's what an editor of the *Saturday Evening Post* once called Mutual of Omaha's Mabel Criss. But Criss, who was noted for her modesty, insisted that her success was due to being part of a great organization.[15]

Criss and her husband, Dr. C. C. Criss, turned the tiny Mutual Benefit Health and Accident Association insurance agency into a major corporation after they bought its charter in 1910. The couple had moved to Omaha from northeastern Nebraska so C.C. could attend Creighton University Medical School.

Mabel began her local career in 1906 by setting up a stenographic service in the Brandeis Building, where her clients included Mutual. After paying $300 for Mutual's charter, Mabel managed the office, and C.C. sold insurance while he studied medicine. He only practiced medicine for a year, then they worked side by side at Mutual until his death in 1952.

As the company grew, Mabel managed personnel and designed the company's rapidly expanding branch offices and its headquarters at Thirty-Third and Farnam Streets. She was second vice president of Mutual from 1928 to 1950 and spent many years as a director and first vice president of United of Omaha, a Mutual of Omaha affiliate.[16]

Criss's role went far beyond her business titles. She became a "work mom" to the generations of young Mutual of Omaha women employees who left their small towns to work for the company, said Elaine Allen, a senior business analyst at Mutual.[17] One woman who joined the company in 1962 called her a "very professional, unique lady who came to work every day, rain or shine . . . she was always dressed in a dress or skirt and jacket and wore her white gloves. In the early days, all the ladies were required to wear white gloves to work."[18]

Criss, who lived in an apartment on the top floor of the original headquarters building, spent time on the floors working with her employees. She wrote dress and professional conduct codes to help them succeed and be safe, said Allen.[19]

After C.C. died, Mabel made two donations to Creighton's medical school totaling about $7 million (equivalent to about $55 million today). In 1963 Creighton named her a founder of the Wisconsin Province of the Jesuits. University officials said that the health science schools had been at risk until these gifts. Today three Creighton medical buildings are named for the Criss family.[20]

A reserved woman who worked for years after normal retirement (but would never reveal her age), Criss also was involved in projects for Children's Hospital, Clarkson Hospital, and the Clarkson School of Nursing. She and Rachel Gallagher were the only two women to serve on the mayor's City-Wide Planning Committee. The Criss Library at the University of Nebraska at Omaha is named for her and her husband. She died in 1978.[21]

Janice Stoney: From Customer Service Representative to Phone Company President

Janice Stoney became a rare exception to the male domination of major Omaha businesses as she rose to the top of the old Northwestern Bell, which later became U.S. West. She followed an unusual path because she was the daughter of a single parent who worked as a secretary, and she didn't even have a college degree.

Instead of going to college after she graduated from Benson High School, Stoney married her husband, Larry. She got a job as a customer service representative for Northwestern Bell to put him through Omaha University. Stoney, now of Phoenix, recalled earning $57 a week for solving customers' problems, ranging from adding services to handling complaints. The job paid well for the early 1960s and normally went to college graduates.[22]

Until about 1970 Stoney still planned to attend college, but the phone company kept promoting her. Before becoming CEO of Northwestern Bell in 1986, she rose through seven layers of management. The phone company also sent her to prestigious professional development programs at places such as the Brookings Institute.[23]

When Stoney became the phone company CEO, she also broke the glass ceilings at the community institutions to which top CEOs belong, such as the Board of Governors of Aksarben. She was its first female member, and people speculated what she would wear to the Aksarben coronation instead of a tuxedo. After AT&T was broken up and Northwestern Bell became part of U.S. West, Stoney became a top executive there. In 1992 she retired as executive vice president of quality for U.S. West.

She and her husband were both politically active. Larry served in the Nebraska Legislature, and she ran unsuccessfully for the U.S. Senate against Bob Kerrey in 1994. Today she serves on numerous corporate boards.

Stoney said that she learned to pick her battles. If a man cut her off during the meeting, she would talk privately to him later.[24] When she became vice president for marketing, her company expected her to join the old Omaha Club, but it banned women from its main dining room. She rejected the "women's membership" it offered but joined as a full member after the Omaha Club changed the discriminatory policy.[25]

Stoney also said it would be hard for a young person to follow her career path of rising through the ranks with one firm because the days of spending a lifetime with one company are gone.[26]

Omaha's Greatest Businesswoman: Mrs. B

Omaha has produced a few business geniuses, such as Warren Buffett, but none greater than Rose Blumkin, "Mrs. B"—the four-foot-ten Russian Jewish immigrant who founded Nebraska Furniture Mart and turned it into a retail behemoth. Riding a scooter and often yelling at her employees in heavily accented English, she sold carpeting until shortly before she died, at age 104, in 1998. Nobel Prize winners might envy the obituary the *Omaha World-Herald* gave her. "She came over here unable to speak the language," said Buffett, who bought the Furniture Mart in 1983. "They'll be studying her in business history books for decades to come."[27]

Today Mrs. B's kingdom sprawls over several acres and blocks on South Seventy-Second Street, with additional mega-stores in Kansas City and Dallas. Drivers navigate through the Omaha complex on a street named after her. On Black Friday and during Buffett's Berkshire Hathaway annual meeting weekends, customers might have trouble finding a parking place in the massive lots.

The legend of Mrs. B began in western Czarist Russia, where Rose Gorelick was one of eight children of a rabbi and his wife. By the time she was sixteen, she was managing a dry goods store in a Russian city. She married her husband, Isadore Blumkin, in 1914.

When World War I broke out, he fled to the United States to avoid fighting in the czar's army. Three years later she took the Trans-Siberian Railroad to the China border and escaped from Russia by promising to bring a guard some vodka but never returned. She reunited with her husband in Fort Dodge, Iowa, before moving, in 1919, to Omaha, where Isadore opened a used clothing store.[28] Mrs. B focused on raising their four children before joining her husband's store in 1932, then opening her own furniture store at 1312 Farnam Street five years later.

Her business credo was "sell cheap, tell the truth, don't cheat nobody." She became famous for the way she built her business. For example, at one point she sold all the furniture and appliances in her own home to get $800 to pay her suppliers, even though her children had to sleep on mattresses on the floor. In 1950 she rented the City Auditorium to pay off a $50,000 bank loan and grossed $250,000 in a three-day sale.[29] Nothing could stop her.

In 1945 the Furniture Mart moved to 2205 Farnam Street, where it remained until 1980, when Mrs. B closed the location to consolidate operations in the massive Seventy-Second Street store that opened in 1970.

When Buffett bought the Furniture Mart in 1983, he paid $60 million. Mrs. B asked that no lawyers or accountants be involved, saying, "I trust you more."[30] Mrs. B worked sixty hours a week and never took vacations. In 1989 she left the Furniture Mart in a dispute over carpet department management with grandsons Ron and Isadore Blumkin, who were running the business. Although she was ninety-five, she opened Mrs. B's Warehouse adjacent to the Mart. A few years later she reconciled with her grandsons and kept selling carpet.[31]

Perhaps one episode best epitomizes the legend of Mrs. B. In the early days a carpet manufacturer took her to court for violating Nebraska's fair trade laws by underselling her competitors. She couldn't afford a lawyer but told the judge, "Why should I charge a higher price? I'm making a fortune as it is." A day after dismissing the case, the judge visited the store and bought $1,400 worth of carpeting.[32]

Blumkin's many accolades included an honorary doctorate in commercial science from New York University; she was the first woman to receive this significant prize. Creighton also awarded her an honorary degree.[33] The Rose Blumkin Performing Arts Center (the renovated Astro Theater) and the Rose Blumkin Home are named for her. She bought the Astro to keep the theater from being torn down because her daughter, Frances Batt, had won a singing contest there. The Rose, as it is commonly called, is home to the former Emmy Gifford Children's Theater.[34]

When Mrs. B died, the store stayed open because her family knew that's what she would want.[35]

A Legacy of Mentoring: Marian Ivers

Like Omaha business, the Greater Omaha Chamber of Commerce was traditionally male dominated, although that has changed. Marian Ivers, who rose from executive secretary to executive vice president, opened doors to women in business by mentoring her employees and creating mentoring programs that are still teaching women how to lead.

Ivers helped found Leadership Omaha, the Institute for Career Advancement Needs (ICAN), and the Women's Fund of Omaha.[36] Connie Spellman, whom Ivers hired to run Leadership Omaha, said that Ivers taught her how to become a confident leader. Spellman later ran Omaha by Design.

"In the mid-1970s women were not respected and valued in career roles as much as men," said Spellman. The few women in most business meetings were often "too intimidated to speak out even when they knew how to solve a problem." Ivers taught confidence by modeling it and exuded competence. "In our little sessions Marian told me to get rid of those thoughts because she said I was as capable of saying what needed to be said as anyone and not to worry whether or not someone liked it," Spellman recalled. Ivers also assigned difficult tasks that subordinates learned to accomplish.[37]

"Marian wanted to constantly do more for the community and Omaha," Spellman said. "She jump-started programs like Leadership Omaha and the Women's Fund because she knew what needed to be done to somewhat equal the playing field with men."[38]

Ivers died in 2013 at age ninety. A conference room in the University of Nebraska at Omaha Barbara Weitz Community Engagement Center is named for her, as is the university's annual community service leadership award.

10

Restaurants and Bakeries

Wherever they came from, Omaha women brought their food with them—everything from kolaches to curry. Many turned their recipes into family restaurant businesses that they ran with their husbands, with "mom" doing the cooking. These places became neighborhood hubs.

Women have run everything from gourmet landmarks in the Old Market to a soul food café so good it made cable TV. A few Omaha women began their careers as bootleggers but transitioned to running family restaurants after Prohibition ended. One popular place, the Italian Gardens, got off to a violent start.

Women Bootleggers Go Respectable

During the 1930s Omaha was swept by racketeering feuds and bombings as residents celebrated the end of Prohibition. The threat of violence especially hung over Little Italy, where many bootleggers had operated and legal bars and restaurants were opening. In 1934, when former bootlegger Giuseppina Marcuzzo prepared to open the Italian Gardens, about four dozen of her neighbors signed a petition to halt the opening due to fears of violence.

Their fears were justified. The day before the scheduled opening, a bomb exploded and littered the restaurant's entrance with bricks. It also destroyed the bar. When Marcuzzo heard the explosion, she ran to the scene and fainted after seeing the damage. Her children carried her home. Since police never charged anyone with the bombing, it's impossible to say who the perpetrator was. However, Marcuzzo repaired the damage and opened a few months later. The Italian Gardens became one of Omaha's most popular restaurants and remained in her family until the 1960s.[1]

The Italian Gardens wasn't the only Italian restaurant with bootlegging roots. The old Trentino's, long one of Omaha's most prominent steakhouses, was founded by Louise Salerno and her husband, Tony, who had both been arrested on Prohibition charges in a 1932 raid on their home. After Prohibition they opened Trentino's, which was noted for its ornate décor and a menu that served steaks with a side of spaghetti (a local trademark).

In 1962, after Tony died, Louise bought the Italian Gardens and ran it until it closed in 1969. In her later life groups overlooked her bootlegging past and honored her for her charitable work. Creighton University, for example, cited her for her kindness to nursing students at St. Joseph's and St. Catherine's Hospitals, near Little Italy, when it presented her with an alumni award.[2]

The Women behind Omaha's Restaurants

Marcuzzo and Salerno were more visible than many women in family restaurants. Most women worked behind the scenes, said Jim Trebbien, retired dean of culinary arts at Metropolitan Community College. They supplied the recipes and ran the kitchens, while their husbands worked out front and managed the business: "People would retire from other professions and if mom knew how to cook, they would make a go in the restaurant business on her favorite recipes."[3] Opening a restaurant was a great business for immigrants because it used to be inexpensive. All it required was a stove, a refrigerator, a steam table, and family members to staff the place.[4] Many restaurant owners were related by birth or marriage. For example, Anthony Piccolo, son of Piccolo Pete's founder, Joseph, married Grace Caniglia, the only daughter of the city's most prominent restaurant clan.[5] While the Caniglia name seemed to be everywhere, the family's greatest contribution might have been using Giovanna Caniglia's recipe to introduce Omaha to pizza after World War II.

The Caniglias

Like many Omaha Italians, Cirno and Giovanna Caniglia emigrated from the town of Carlentini, Sicily. Cirno, who operated a bakery, delivered fresh bread to restaurants every morning. That changed after World War II because their son, Eli, had eaten a new dish called "pizza" in a Baltimore restaurant while waiting to go overseas. It reminded him of his mother's *cucurene*, a double-crusted meat-and-cheese pastry. "We could make a fortune with something called pizza," he wrote his father.

In August 1946 the Caniglias opened an addition to their bakery at Seventh and Pierce Streets and called it a pizzeria. But first they had to teach customers how to eat the new dish. The pizzeria was the first of numerous popular restaurants that the family's five sons and grandchildren opened over the next fifty years. Others included Venice Inn, Mister C's, the Italian Steakhouse, Luigi's, and Top of the World. Although most have since closed, some became local legends, especially Mr. C's, which was decorated year-round with thousands of Christmas lights.[6] Children left with balloons that owner Yano Caniglia twisted into animals.

Other Multigenerational Family Restaurants

Ethnic restaurants are woven into Omaha's DNA, although many old favorites have closed. Czech immigrants Josef and Ann Libor ran the Bohemian Café, on South Thirteenth Street, whose servers wore Czech costumes with red skirts and embroidered blouses. The menu featured dumplings, sauerkraut, beer, and Czech pastries such as kolaches. Their family ran the Bohemian until it closed in 2016.[7] Before it closed, customers lined up outside for two blocks to get a final serving of dumplings and sauerkraut.

However, other longtime family restaurants have survived. For example, Frank Kawa's granddaughters Kari and Sally now operate South Omaha's premier steakhouse, Johnny's Café, adjacent to the old Stockyards. Kawa, a Polish immigrant, bought the sandwich shop and bar in 1922 and turned it into a restaurant where cattlemen who had just taken livestock to market and business leaders in suits were equally common. During Prohibition Kawa sold beer, but federal agents could never pin anything on him, said his son, Jack Kawa.[8]

The Fair Deal and Big Mama's

Neighborhood places often reflect the area's ethnic identity. On the African American Near North Side, the Fair Deal Café, at 2118 North Twenty-Fourth Street, became known as Omaha's Black City Hall. During the civil rights era, community leaders gathered there to discuss issues as they devoured fried chicken, greens, sweet potato pie, and other soul food specialties.

Owner Charles Hall partnered with his wife, Audentria (Dennie), who cooked breakfast while he handled dinner. After she fell ill in 1996 and died from her injuries, Hall told journalist Leo Adam Biga that he was bereft without her there "looking over my shoulder and telling me what to do."[9]

Another local soul food restaurant, Big Mama's Kitchen, became nationally famous after the Food Network and Travel Channel featured it numerous times. Patricia "Big Mama" Barron opened the restaurant at Forty-Fifth and Bedford Streets in 2007, after retiring from telecommunications. Barron rose from being a key-punch operator to upper management in U.S. West Communications. On the side she studied culinary arts at Metropolitan Community College.

When she opened her restaurant, featuring fried chicken and other soul food specialties, she brought her children and grandchildren into the business. But her larger goal was to help restore vibrancy to the North Omaha community, said her daughter, Gladys Harrison, who became the restaurant's general manager. "My mom didn't just want to own a restaurant . . . She wanted a place where everybody in the city could come and get together," she said after her mother died in 2018. The Food Network even considered basing a reality TV show there but abandoned the project for lack of drama. The restaurant has since moved to the Highlander Accelerator Building at Thirtieth and Parker Streets.[10]

As Omaha grew more sophisticated during the 1960s and 1970s, many residents longed for gourmet food such as they found elsewhere. Women opened some of the signature restaurants that turned the Old Market from a hippie haven to a major tourist attraction.

M's Stands for Mary—and Mellen

It took a few years after the produce warehouses closed for the Old Market to emerge as Omaha's most popular center of nightlife. For a time the area became a haven for hippies and drug users, but Mary Vogel had a vision of the district's potential when she opened the elegant M's Pub at Eleventh and Howard Streets in 1972, said Tony Abbott, owner of the equally elegant nearby French Café. This vision led Vogel to take a chance on the Old Market and to introduce Omaha to a new style of dining. Her menu featured cucumber sandwiches, homemade soups, shish kebab sandwiches, and lavosh.[11]

"M's altered the fate of the neighborhood around its spot at Eleventh and Howard Streets. It changed the way Omahans ate and socialized," wrote World-Herald food critic Sarah Baker Hansen. "It convinced our city and its visitors that yes, we knew good food, but damn, we also knew atmosphere."[12] After Vogel sold

M's to Ann Mellen's parents in 1979, she volunteered for cultural groups until her death in 2000.[13]

Mellen, M's second founding mother, bought M's from her parents in 1984 in partnership with Ron Samuelson. In 1993 she opened Vivace's, another elegant Old Market restaurant that has since closed.

On January 9, 2016, a gas explosion destroyed M's and other adjacent properties, leaving only the exterior brick walls standing. There were questions about whether the buildings could survive, but Mellen announced that M's would come back. For months sidewalks were blocked by scaffolding as Mellen worked with architects to restore the pub to its original state. Its reopening on November 1, 2017, was the talk of the city.[14] "Omaha's M's Pub is back," wrote Hansen in a column celebrating the event. There were small differences such as the move of the restrooms and part of the kitchen from the basement to the main floor, but much remained "exactly the same." M's Pub again anchors the Market's central corner.

Other more modest restaurants, bakeries and bars too numerous to mention, anchor other neighborhoods throughout Omaha. Some, such as Gerda's German Restaurant, have been run by colorful owners like the beloved Gerda Bailey, a German immigrant who ran this Aksarben / Elmwood Park institution until she died in 2018.

From Germany to Midtown: Gerda's German Restaurant

"Sorry We're Closed," said the sign on Gerda's German Restaurant at Fifty-First and Leavenworth Streets in 2018. The Midtown Omaha institution was no longer dispensing fresh doughnuts, orange Danish, cinnamon rolls, and several kinds of rye bread. No more would regular customers sit on their regular stools around a U-shaped counter, serving themselves coffee as they devoured the morning paper along with their glazed twists.

Bailey had died, and customers mourned losing both her and her bakery.

Bailey, who was born in Augsburg, Germany, in 1935, spent much of her childhood hiding from Allied bombs. After the war she met John Bailey, an American soldier. They married and had two sons, before he was transferred to Fayetteville, North Carolina.

Gerda began baking wedding cakes while working for a grocery store there. After divorcing Bailey, she married an airman who failed to tell her that he had been married to a Korean woman and had fathered a daughter. When a social worker told Gerda about the girl, she picked her up and adopted her. Gerda came to Omaha when her husband was assigned to Offutt Air Force Base but divorced him in 1976 and kept their daughter, Kim.

At that time she opened her restaurant-bakery. It became a fixture in Midtown for both its baked goods and for Bailey's generosity and love of fun. Bailey and a friend who was a nun often visited the Council Bluffs casinos. She also took friends to Germany, started the bakery's Oktoberfest celebrations, and donated food and money to numerous charities and individuals. Unfortunately, because she did not own her building, she could not sell her business, so it closed after her death in 2018. She was eighty-three when she died and had worked almost until then.[15]

The Cycle Continues

Omaha's newest residents continue to contribute to the city's diverse culinary offerings. Downtown South Omaha is packed with family-run Mexican restaurants, and at strip malls around the city, patrons can sample Ethiopian, Sudanese, and other African cuisines. Some are attached to ethnic grocery stores selling the ingredients for Indian, Thai, and other Asian and African food. The descendants of Omahans who got addicted to pizza after World War II can now satisfy a craving for Moroccan couscous or Ethiopian injera bread. The cycle continues.

11

Sports

The golden age of women's sports began when federal Title IX opened athletic opportunities to high school and college females in the 1970s. Long before then, however, Omaha produced outstanding women athletes, including a national cycling champion in 1889. Nebraska offered few high school or college sports for girls until the late 1960s, when Connie Claussen of the University of Nebraska at Omaha (UNO) and Mary Higgins of Creighton University started outstanding intercollegiate programs at their schools. Today crowds fill gyms for girls' state championships just as Omahans packed a cycling arena to cheer their own Lillie Williams on to a national championship during the Gilded Age.

Omaha Woman Cycles to Championship in 1889

On the last night of a tense six-day race in 1889, a capacity crowd filled Omaha's new cycling coliseum to cheer on local sensation Lillie Williams in a national women's cycling competition. Fans paid fifty cents a ticket—double the usual price—to see the final three hours of the cumulative eighteen-hour race, which the *Omaha Bee* proclaimed the most interesting sporting event that Omaha had ever witnessed.[1]

Williams, who was soon dubbed "the Nebraska Cyclone," did not disappoint the thirty thousand spectators who packed the coliseum to overflowing for the week. Not only did she sprint fast enough to make up time lost during a crash on the third night; she set the women's eighteen-hour cycling record and won a gold medal.[2] The next year she was named the national women's cycling champion after winning another six-night race in Omaha.[3] She quit her job in the *Omaha Bee*'s composing room for a successful career in professional cycling.[4]

Williams was a product of the national cycling boom that began in the 1870s and was Omaha's first successful woman athlete. She remained a rarity for nearly a century, until the federal Title IX legislation opened sports to widespread female participation. Her chosen sport was not an accident. Bicycling gave women so much freedom of movement that suffragist leader Susan B. Anthony said it had "done more to emancipate women than anything else in the world."[5]

Spectators were fascinated by the sight of women in racing costumes of tights with close-fitting jackets or jerseys and colorful sashes and caps.[6] Women's races were often treated more as spectacles than serious sports, as they sometimes raced against men and even horses and greyhounds.[7] Their sport was controversial because it flaunted conventional ideas of female fragility. In 1894 the sports magazine *Referee* said it robbed competitors of "almost all visible attributes that we commonly associate with womankind," outraging "true gentlemen." In the mid-1890s cycling's governing body refused to sanction races involving women.[8]

Williams left Omaha after her early races but continued to compete as long as tracks continued to hire women. Eventually, she became a national fencing champion and competed in swimming and motorcycle racing.[9]

After Williams's groundbreaking success, competitive local sports for women almost disappeared until the 1970s, although country clubs sponsored golf and tennis tournaments for both genders. At the turn of the last century, high schools and colleges offered a few competitive sports for women locally as well as nationally, but the University of Nebraska played an important role in their virtual disappearance.

Birth of Women's Sports

Despite formidable obstacles, such as worries over modesty and fears of damaging their reproductive systems, women nationally began competing in a few sports during the late nineteenth century. Some elite colleges offered competitive women's basketball in the 1890s and spread the sport to high schools. The University of Nebraska had a varsity women's basketball team, but men could not attend games in which women played in long bloomers. Other early women's sports included croquet, gymnastics, swimming, and even track and field, while rich women played golf and tennis.[10]

"Americans were more restrictive [of women in sports] than Europeans," said Dr. Benjamin Rader, professor emeritus of history at the University of Nebraska–Lincoln. In 1900 twenty-two women competed in golf, tennis, and croquet at the Paris Olympics, the first Olympics open to women.[11] In 1926, 65 women out of 2,561 total athletes participated in the Antwerp Olympics in several sports, including swimming and diving.[12] However, one of the fiercest opponents of such competition was a Nebraskan.

Impact of Mabel Lee

Mabel Lee, chair of the Department of Physical Education for Women at the University of Nebraska from 1924 to 1952, was a formidable opponent of women's competitive sports. As the first woman president of the American Association of Health, Physical Education, and Recreation and the American Academy of Physical Education, she opposed the male competitive athletic model.[13] She persuaded the Athletic Conference of American College Women to oppose all varsity competition for women.[14]

"Her view was that women's sports shouldn't emphasize winning at all costs. She placed more stress on universal participation
and did not like elite sports. She had a point there," said Radar.
Nebraska high schools dropped girls' varsity sports, although
nearby Iowa retained its strong varsity female sports programs,
including its popular six-player version of basketball.[15] In 1977
the Women's Physical Education Building at the University of
Nebraska–Lincoln was renamed Mabel Lee Hall.[16] Despite Lee's
influence, Omaha offered women a few opportunities to compete in country club sports like golf and tennis. That's how Jann
Walker Thomas nearly became a professional golfer and got to
know Arnold Palmer.

Jann Walker Thomas: Golfing with Arnold Palmer

During the 1950s, when she was one of the two best amateur
women golfers in Nebraska, Jann Walker Thomas went to Lincoln to play a round with a charismatic young golf professional
who was barnstorming around the country to earn a living—
Arnold Palmer.

Palmer, who was "just getting started in professional golf," had
asked his hosts for a good partner, and they recommended Jann
because she had a "good reputation" in state amateur golf circles,
said her husband, Lawrence "Red" Thomas. After that, whenever Palmer came to Nebraska, he would ask to play with Jann.[17]

Thomas grew up in the Elmwood Park area, where she could
use her neighbors' tennis courts, swimming pools, and other facilities. Her father, prominent Omaha insurance executive Richard
Walker, taught her to play golf at the Omaha Country Club when
she was a child. When she was nine, she won her first tournament there, the only female participant. The country club's professionals recognized her talent and gave her free lessons.

Golf and tennis were among the few sports in the 1950s to
offer competitions for women. But only affluent women generally

played these sports, and ordinary women could not enter tournaments that were held at country clubs. As Jann was graduating from Brownell Hall in 1954, she was such a good golfer that the Swanson family (of Swanson Foods) offered to sponsor her to turn pro on the new national women's tour. Using the relatively primitive equipment of that era, she could drive a ball 269 feet. However, her father would not allow her to join the tour and sent her to college instead.[18]

Jann said this was fine with her because by then she had fallen in love with Lawrence "Red" Thomas, who graduated from Central High and later became an executive with ConAgra. She went to college and became Queen of Aksarben in addition to winning two state championships, before marrying Red. She retired from competitive golf in 1961 to raise the family's two children.[19] "I loved being an athlete," she said, "but when my father told me that I could not be a pro, I was in love with Red and that was that. I thought that probably marriage is my mission."[20]

Twenty years later Omaha women would not have to choose between college and sports as Connie Claussen and Mary Higgins created athletic programs at the University of Nebraska at Omaha and Creighton University even before the federal Title IX legislation. After Title IX, high schools and colleges sponsored women's teams in numerous sports, and colleges offered scholarships to women athletes.

Creating Varsity Sports: Connie Clausen and Mary Higgins

Claussen and Higgins, both self-described tomboys who grew up in the Benson area, regretted their lack of athletic opportunities at Benson High School and Marian High School, respectively. They set out to change the situation.

"There were almost zero athletics at Marian," said Higgins, who graduated in 1969 and became its president in 2014. "The only way you could earn a trophy in that era was in debate, speech, or Field Day."[21] Tennis was Benson's only competitive sport for girls, but Claussen became a national table tennis champion for the Benson Community Center.[22]

Claussen, who graduated from Omaha University, began teaching physical education there in 1963. Higgins pushed Creighton to create a sports program for females as an undergraduate during the early 1970s. After graduating in 1973 with a degree in American studies, she worked in admissions, then moved to athletics in 1975. Both infant programs were bolstered by Title IX, which required schools to offer women's sports.

From the Quonset Hut to Connie Claussen Field

In 1973 Claussen rebelled against teaching physical education courses and voluntarily coaching the varsity softball and volleyball teams she had created. She said that from then on, she would only teach her classes and no longer coach for free. It was bad enough that UNO housed women's athletics in a Quonset hut with no showers, but males got paid to coach, not just for teaching. The university paid for men's uniforms, not the alumni association, and teams playing different sports did not share the same uniforms, as women did.[23]

After the *World-Herald* carried a story about Claussen's rebellion and a picture of the Quonset hut, things began to improve. UNO athletic director Don Leahy fought for funds for women's athletics, and Claussen received funding for coaches and some scholarships. In 1980 her program moved to a new physical education building. No longer did she have to purchase uniforms at the bookstore, and each team got its own uniforms.[24] However, women's sports were still not treated as well as men's. For example, when Claussen won her first national softball championship in 1975, the alumni association, not the university, bought the team's rings.

Claussen eventually gave up coaching softball to devote her-

self full-time to administering women's sports. During one six-
or seven-year period, UNO added five women's sports. It also
won National Collegiate Athletic Association (NCAA) Division II
national championships in soccer, volleyball, and softball.[25] Top
officials such as the late chancellor Del Weber boosted Clauss-
en's programs and the old Women's Walk for Athletics, in which
hundreds of walkers collected pledges for women's athletics. The
walks raised $3 million for UNO's women's sports teams over the
seven years beginning in 1986. Today Claussen advises UNO as
athletic director emerita, and UNO's new baseball and softball
field is named for her.[26]

Mary Higgins: Women Join the Bluejays

When Mary Higgins and her future husband, attorney Patrick
Kennison, were students, he had coached her intramural basketball team, Plum Rum, named for his favorite racehorse.[27] But
Higgins wanted Creighton to offer women more than intramural sports.

During her senior year Higgins and a few others asked assistant athletic director Dan Offenburger if they could start a softball
team that competed with other colleges. After he agreed, Higgins called area colleges, put together a schedule, and the team
drove to games in their personal vehicles wearing makeshift uniforms. The women had no funding, but they were varsity athletes. It was at least a start.

After graduating, Higgins joined Creighton's Office of Admissions before becoming women's intramurals director. Offenburger
asked her to coach varsity softball despite her protest that she
didn't know how. "You'll figure it out," he told her.[28] And she did.

Higgins was so dedicated to her team that she and Kennison
spent their honeymoon at a softball tournament in Fort Dodge,
Iowa, so she could scout prospective players. Her dedication
produced results.

Between 1975 and 1992 Higgins, who also has a master's degree in physical education from UNO, built a Division I program that played in the Women's College World Series and attracted some of the nation's best players, despite Creighton's modest scholarship budget. These top players included Jean Tierney, an all-American second baseman, who is the aunt of retired Minnesota Twins star Joe Mauer.

Initially, Higgins recruited her players at Iowa softball tournaments because of the state's strong high school girls' sports programs. Her husband and eventually their son, daughter, and mother-in-law/nanny accompanied her. However, as softball grew, Higgins was required to recruit year-round at tournaments nationwide. When the combination of recruiting and family became too difficult to juggle, she left coaching for administrative jobs in the Athletic Department. Eventually, she became Creighton's retention director, before retiring in 2014. Soon after, she became president of Marian High School.[29] "I'm proud that we [Creighton] started with nothing and became nationally competitive," she said. "We ranked in the top ten numerous times and participated in the Women's College World Series."[30]

Title IX Opens High School Athletics to Omaha Girls

Before Title IX passed in 1973, Nebraska schools, including those in Omaha, had few team sports for girls, but that changed a year later, when the Nebraska School Activities Association (NSAA) held state championships in volleyball and swimming and diving, said Debra Velder, retired associate director of NSAA. During her forty-seven years with the organization, Velder oversaw the implementation of Title IX statewide.[31]

Other sports followed. In 1975 NSAA added girls' basketball, track and field, and cross-country to its state championships and eventually softball and soccer. By 2019 well over half of Nebraska's high school girls played at least one high school sport.[32]

Velder recalled the difficulties of creating the state's girls' sports programs, including the fact that manufacturers did not produce uniforms for females. Men got most of the coaching jobs because women were not trained for them. In the Omaha Public Schools (OPS) it was difficult to find resources to fund girls' sports. At some schools many female students had difficulty participating in sports because they needed to work after school. Some OPS high schools began unofficially specializing in particular sports. For example, Central High became noted for its female basketball teams, while Burke excelled in swimming and volleyball.

Omaha's Catholic schools also developed excellent girls' teams. One year, for example, all-girl Marian won state championships in five sports, half of the sports then holding state championship competitions.[33] Class B Skutt Catholic also became an athletic powerhouse.

Velder said that the growth of privately run select teams for the best athletes has hurt participation in high school sports. More of them focus on their best sport at an early age, with fewer competing in two or three sports.

Omaha area high schools have produced a number of the female athletes on an *Omaha World-Herald* listing of Nebraska's top one hundred athletes. They are Angee Henry of Bellevue West (track and field), Maurtice Ivy of Omaha Central (basketball), Kelly Lindsey of Millard North (soccer), Alice Schmidt of Elkhorn High (track and field), and Allison Weston, of Papillion-LaVista (volleyball).[34]

Postwar to the Women's Movement

During the 1950s cattle trucks still lined up on South Omaha streets waiting to enter the massive stockyards where thousands worked in the packinghouses. Twenty years later the trucks were gone and most of the packinghouse workers with them. Instead, more Omahans held white-collar jobs in the corporate offices of Union Pacific Railroad, Northwestern Bell Telephone Company, Northern Natural Gas, First National Bank, and Mutual of Omaha and early tech firms such as First Data Resources.[1]

Omaha was growing and changing. Its diverse economy sheltered it from the worst national downturns. Douglas County's population rose from about 280,000 in 1950 to about 540,000 in 1970.[2] Meanwhile, Offutt Air Force Base employed thousands of military and civilian personnel at Strategic Air Command headquarters, and the U.S. Air Force installed a sophisticated telecommunications infrastructure that made Omaha a center of the new telemarketing industry.

During the 1950s Omaha adopted a home rule charter with a strong mayor and city council, replacing the city commission form of government. However, all was not rosy. The city's struggle over civil rights during the 1960s and 1970s was marked by outbreaks of rioting as it grappled with racism and segregation in housing and schools.

The interstate destroyed the old North and South Omaha neighborhoods in its path while boosting the growth of West Omaha. Downtown stores moved to malls in suburban areas. People deserted the downtown after work unless they were headed to one of the boutiques, gourmet restaurants, or wine bars in the newly chic Old Market.

During the 1970s redeveloping the riverfront was deemed key to revitalizing downtown. The old warehouses of Jobber's Canyon gave way to the ConAgra campus as surviving historic buildings were converted into offices and condominiums. Omaha developed a new skyline, and its downtown began attracting young professionals to the apartments and condos in converted stores and warehouses.

Women also were changing. As baby boomer women entered the workforce in record numbers, they complained of job discrimination and glass ceilings. The 1960 U.S. Census showed that women were clustered in lower-status jobs compared with men. Although more than a third of Omaha's workers were female, they mostly held clerical and service jobs or worked in retail or hospitals.[3] Even though the 1964 Civil Rights Act outlawed sex discrimination, enforcement was difficult.

In 1967 the city formed the Mayor's Commission on the Status of Women, which sought changes in the roles of women in everything from business to social services and sports. However, the commission lacked power to make such changes, and it drew fire from those who opposed them. After his 1977 election, Mayor Al Veys demanded changes in the way the commission operated that led to its demise. But this could not halt the progress of women.

Baby boomer women, who grew up expecting equal opportunities, became doctors, lawyers, corporate managers, police officers, firefighters, and reporters. Discrimination against women became major local news, which helped bring changes. The public schools stopped firing teachers when they became pregnant, and women started winning local elections. Cracks appeared in the glass ceilings in nearly all fields. Like the rest of the nation, Omaha would never be the same. And in the 1990s the privately run Omaha Women's Fund began conducting research on issues facing women and worked to fund and empower women and women's groups.

12

Law

Although there have been women lawyers in Omaha since the 1890s, job discrimination limited their numbers until the modern era. Most of the early women lawyers practiced in family firms with their fathers or husbands because other firms would not hire them.[1] The women who finally broke the barriers tended to be outstanding and sometimes were appointed judges. They also worked in public law positions or family businesses, where their legal backgrounds were helpful.

When the women's movement came, women flocked to legal careers, some with the idea of fighting gender and/or racial discrimination. Now law classes at the University of Nebraska–Lincoln and Creighton University are at least half-female. Most of these students are too young to believe there was a time when Eleanor Knoll Swanson was the only woman in the National Moot Court competition.

Eleanor Knoll Swanson: Trailblazing Attorney

"Nebraska defeats Georgetown for National Championship!" That was the startling news at the University of Nebraska Law School in 1953 as its Moot Court team defeated Georgetown in a national competition in New York—and the hero was the only woman in the tournament, Eleanor Knoll Swanson of Omaha. Swanson, a twenty-nine-year-old former teacher, delivered her closing argument in the finals before a panel of judges that included Supreme Court justice Tom Clark.[2]

Years later Swanson's teammate, Omaha attorney Ronald Hunter, said Swanson gave the best argument in the country that year, and he called her "a phenomenal gal."[3] She was also a groundbreaking female attorney in Omaha, recalled Richard Shugrue, professor emeritus of law at Creighton University. For years she was one of only two Omaha women practicing in a law firm.[4]

Swanson worked for the Justice Department in Washington DC after she graduated from law school but later returned to Omaha. In 1961 she joined Margaret Fisher in a general practice law firm.[5] Fifteen years later, when the Omaha Business and Professional Women's Club named her Woman of the Year, she was practicing with Green, Marshall and Green.[6] She was noted for her efforts to reform Nebraska adoption laws as well as her mentorship of other women lawyers. "She took me under her wing and was a really good mentor to me," said Lynne Timmerman Fees. Many groups honored her work in advancing women in the legal field, including the Nebraska Bar Association, North High School, and the University of Nebraska.[7]

Swanson "always followed her own path," said her daughter, Katherine Valentino of Fairfax, Virginia, when her mother died in 2009. Her *World-Herald* obituary hailed her as a "trailblazer."[8] "She was the go-to woman lawyer in Omaha," said Shugrue.[9]

Barriers to Early Women in Law

Swanson's trailblazing career followed decades in which women in Omaha and elsewhere struggled to practice law. Unlike health care, there was no woman-friendly occupation such as nursing or hospital administration to give women access to the world of legal work. In states like Illinois, women couldn't become lawyers because they couldn't vote, and being able to vote was a requirement for practicing law.[10] Although Nebraska did not have such a requirement, State Bar Association records show that during the 1880s and 1890s only twenty-three women were admitted to the state bar and just two of them, Thea Elliott and Mae C. Wood, were from Douglas County.[11]

Originally, prospective lawyers studied in law offices, but that changed after 1891, when the University of Nebraska took over an informal Lincoln law college.[12] In 1903 Roscoe Pound became dean of the University of Nebraska Law College, which had graduated its first woman in 1892. He reformed its curriculum and added a third year of study. Creighton's Law School opened in 1904, and graduated its first woman seven years later.[13]

Pound moved first to Northwestern University in 1907, then to Harvard Law School, where he gained national fame serving as dean from 1916 to 1936. A poem he wrote for the 1905 university yearbook predicted the future of women in law:

BACK TO THE FARM MEN
It's all off now.
Back to the shovel,
Back to the plow.
Before judge and court
You'll stand no show.
Woman's time is here.
Man had better go
As co-eds increase
Three-fold each year,
Law will soon become
A woman's sphere.[14]

However, both Nebraska law schools seldom included more than one or two women per class until the 1970s. Problems began in the classroom with law school professors who were accustomed to dealing with men and used foul language that tended to offend women. Many professors did not think women belonged in law. "Those who survived were tough and determined," said Shugrue, a Nebraska law alumnus. Hiring discrimination kept women from getting jobs in non–family law firms. Often they worked in public law or businesses related to the law.[15] Nationally, discrimination against women lawyers was equally rampant. The late Supreme Court justice Ruth Bader Ginsburg could not get a job with a New York law firm despite having graduated at the top of her class from Columbia University Law School.

In Omaha a few pioneering women attorneys in addition to Swanson began to break the gender barriers. They included judges Elizabeth Davis Pittman and Colleen Buckley as well as Rosemary Skrupa, a member of the boards of the Omaha Public Power District and University of Nebraska Regents.[16] All helped pave the way for the influx of women into the field of law during the 1970s.

Judge Elizabeth Davis Pittman

Pittman was the first female African American to graduate from Creighton's School of Law in 1948. Her father, Charles Davis, was an Omaha attorney who had opened one of the nation's first Black-owned savings and loan associations. In 1950 she was one of only thirty-nine African American women lawyers nationally.[17]

Pittman also was the first Black and first female deputy county attorney in Douglas County and the first African American elected to the Omaha School Board. In 1971 Governor J.J. Exon appointed her a municipal court judge, Nebraska's first Black and first female judge. Later she became a county judge. After retiring from the court in 1986, she became a legal advisor in a firm run by Don Kleine, longtime Douglas County attorney.

Pittman, who died in 1998, was a leader in groups such as the National Federation of Settlements and Neighborhood Centers, the YWCA, and the Governor's Commission on the Status of Women.[18] That year Creighton University marked the fiftieth anniversary of her graduation by naming the Elizabeth Davis Pittman Building in her honor. Today it also presents the Elizabeth Pittman Award to African American law graduates who mirror her excellence, perseverance, and dedication. "She knew the law very well and gave everybody a fair shake," said Kleine.[19] Among Pittman's judicial colleagues was juvenile judge Colleen Buckley.

Judge Colleen Buckley

Buckley, a native of LeMars, Iowa, taught in Illinois, Iowa, and Nebraska and was a social worker before graduating from Creighton Law School in 1962. She became a Legal Aid attorney and worked in the Douglas County Attorney's office before Governor Exon appointed her to the juvenile court in 1972. She served there for twenty-two years, then joined Boys Town, mentoring young people.

"She combined the behavior of a strict judge with a heart of gold," said the Reverend Val Peter, former executive director of Boys Town, in 1998, after Buckley died. "There are many alumni of Boys Town who are very, very grateful." In 1994 Boys Town presented her with its prestigious Spirit of Youth Award, previously given to luminaries such as Saint Teresa of Calcutta.[20]

Rosemary Skrupa

Like Buckley, Rosemary Skrupa was a teacher before becoming a lawyer. However, she was best known for running a law-based business and holding elected office. Skrupa graduated from Duchesne College and taught in Omaha public and parochial schools before entering Creighton Law School. She started her law career as a deputy county attorney for Hall County in her hometown, Grand Island.[21]

For forty years Skrupa and her husband, Frank, ran Credit Advisors, a credit counseling company that helped consumers defend themselves against creditors. Rosemary Skrupa also helped write laws on credit counseling nationally. She became an acting municipal court judge in 1979 and served until 1983.[22]

Skrupa was elected to the Omaha Public Power District (OPPD) in 1974 and, in 1988, to the University of Nebraska Board of Regents, where she served until 2000. She was OPPD's first elected woman member and its first woman president. On the board of regents she advocated for the University of Nebraska at Omaha and the University of Nebraska Medical Center. She died in 2013.[23]

Groundbreakers Succeed

The women's movement drastically changed the demographics of the legal profession in Nebraska and nationally. Not only do about equal numbers of women and men graduate from the state's local law schools; they find jobs in all types of law, including Omaha's major corporate law firms. They hold judgeships at all levels of the state and local courts, including the Nebraska Supreme Court. Professor Marianne Culhane was Creighton University School of Law's first woman dean.

13

Government

For years local government was virtually a boy's club, with no women on the city council until Betty Abbott was elected in 1965. There were no women on the Douglas County Board until Carole Woods Harris and Bernice Labedz were elected in 1992. Men headed all the city departments until 1977, when Ruth Jackson became Human Relations Department director. They also dominated most of the powerful advisory boards, and there were no female police officers or firefighters.[1] Jean Stothert became Omaha's first woman mayor in 2013.

But even before women routinely began winning local government elections, several women held important appointive and administrative posts, including Rachel Gallagher of the Parks Department and city clerk Mary Galligan Cornett. These women, along with Betty Abbott, opened doors for women in city government.

Omaha City Government

Betty Abbott Breaks into the Boy's Club

For about a dozen minutes in 1978, a who's who of Omaha stomped, clapped, and pounded tables at Peony Park Ballroom, stopping the Omaha Press Club Show as a tall blonde in a shimmering gown sauntered onto the stage to sing about her defeat for mayor. "Who's sorry now? Who cast a vote they're regretting somehow?"

At the sound of Betty Abbott's torch singer voice, applause broke out and continued for five minutes as the audience realized that Abbott, the first woman to run for mayor, was playing herself in the annual spoof of local politics. When she resumed singing, people stomped their feet, pounded tables, and clapped for seven more minutes. Later Abbott called the moment "phenomenal" but focused on the future, not her electoral loss.[2]

Abbott, who was elected to the city council in 1965, served for twelve years before running for mayor in 1977. She is credited with helping save and restore the Orpheum Theater, helping gain national recognition for the Henry Doorly Zoo, sponsoring city air pollution control legislation, working with Rachel Gallagher and Friends of the Parks to keep UNO from building a parking lot in the Elmwood Park ravine, and fighting to keep Midtown neighborhoods intact.[3]

However, her first election made some men nervous. Omaha council president H. F. Jacobberger confessed his worry that "having a woman in city government is going to be murder" but later admitted his mistake.[4]

Abbott, who was noted both for her mastery of complex issues and her affability, was born in Council Bluffs, Iowa, and began her career in radio in Des Moines, after studying music at Drake University. She continued her radio career after moving to Omaha in 1949, working for several stations. As television became more popular, she started the TV *Babysitter*, a Saturday morning show for children.[5]

She got involved in politics through the League of Women Voters before running unsuccessfully for city council in 1961. When she ran again, in 1965, she won, partially due to a scandal that led to the indictment of Mayor James Dworak. Voters thought a woman would be a reformer.

Abbott ran for mayor against fellow council member Al Veys of South Omaha in 1977 in an election that many thought was influenced by sexism, even though voters elected Mary Kay Green to the city council. Green, a member of a prominent Democratic family and an outspoken feminist, served one term.

After Abbott lost the mayor's race, she started a new business, coped with the death of her husband, Doug, and got involved in new projects to improve urban Omaha.[6] These included promoting vocational education and state economic development, in addition to boosting the arts and working to improve downtown Omaha. President Gerald Ford appointed her to the U.S. Defense Department's commission on women. And she was praised for breaking ground for women in politics.

After Abbott's death, in 2005, the *World-Herald* said her council service and run for mayor "set the stage for other women to become involved in Omaha politics."[7]

During the first years when Abbott was one of the first women in City Hall, she had company in the Parks Department—Rachel Gallagher, who made an unpaid career out of protecting and improving Omaha's parks.

Rachel Gallagher: Powerful Crusader for Parks

When Rachel Gallagher resigned from the Parks and Recreation Advisory Board, in 1968, news accounts described her as the person who had done more for Omaha's parks than anyone else.[8] An urban legend held that she had threatened to chain herself to a tree to protect Elmwood Park from University of Nebraska at Omaha (UNO) expansion, although this was probably just a rumor. Gallagher had served as chairman of the Parks and Recreation Commission in 1950 and later served on the Parks and Recreation Advisory Board, exercising great power over the city's park system.[9]

The colorful Kansas City native who met her husband, Paul, at Lake Okoboji, Iowa, when she was a student at Smith College, became one of Omaha's best-known citizens. Paul's wealthy family owned Paxton & Gallagher wholesale grocers, which produced Butternut Coffee and was later sold to Coca-Cola. After their 1915 wedding, the Gallaghers moved into his family's Gold Coast mansion, where they lived for years.[10] Rachel never had to clean house or cook and got involved in volunteer work after co-founding the Junior League in 1919.

Gallagher began fighting to expand and beautify Omaha's parks after reading a library book on architectural landscaping.[11] In 1936 she joined the Omaha City Improvement Council and became president in 1940. For the next six years she attended every meeting of any sort that she saw in the newspaper in order to promote improving Omaha. Her trademark was relentless persistence.

In 1946 Gallagher and Mabel Criss, of Mutual of Omaha, were the only two women named to the mayor's City-Wide Planning Committee. Gallagher became chair of the Parks, Playgrounds, and Recreation Division and was appointed to a four-year term on the Parks and Recreation Commission. She also led the search for a full-time parks department administrator and co-founded Friends of the Parks, turning it into a powerful force.[12]

Nothing intimidated this small, stylish woman who always wore a hat. For example, when interstate highway construction during the 1950s threatened five city parks, including Elmwood and Riverview (now the Henry Doorly Zoo & Aquarium), she lobbied the Nebraska Legislature to protect them. In addition, she flew to Washington DC and persuaded the U.S. secretary of commerce to prevent the state Highway Department from taking park land without the secretary's written permission.[13]

In the late 1960s, when UNO threatened to expand into Elmwood Park, Gallagher spearheaded the opposition.[14] UNO expanded westward instead, even though this meant taking over a number of large homes and turning them into offices. Gallagher and her husband also raised money to convert the old Krug Amusement Center at Fifty-Second and Military into a park that was renamed Gallagher Park in their honor.[15] She also was highly involved in creating the 1957 city charter and winning its public approval.[16]

Gallagher employed three secretaries to help manage all of her unpaid work on boards.[17] While her major focus was the parks, she assisted many other groups. Newspapers described her as a "tireless," "indefatigable" "woman of action" who loved wearing red and refused to wear black. Her hobbies included writing, bowling, and golf, and she was a boxing fan.[18]

Gallagher slowed down after suffering a stroke in 1967 while getting ready to attend a party in California. She recovered, but in July 1970 she suffered another stroke while driving her golf cart at the Omaha Country Club. She suffered several more strokes before dying in her sleep on July 15, 1977.[19]

Margaret Hitchcock Doorly Transforms the Zoo

Gallagher protected Riverview Park's tiny zoo from the interstate highway, but Margaret Hitchcock Doorly transformed it from the equivalent of a menagerie into a real zoo by donating $750,000 ($6.1 million today) the year before she died.

The daughter of *World-Herald* founder, Gilbert Hitchcock, and widow of the newspaper's publisher, Henry Doorly, Margaret was a lifelong animal lover. During the Trans-Mississippi Exposition she rode a bear and camels and allowed a boa constrictor to wrap itself around her arm. Later she rode elephants at zoos in London and Colorado Springs and a tortoise at the Bronx Zoo.[20]

Riverview Park had had a tiny zoo since its opening in 1897. However, the zoo had languished for decades, and in the 1950s it had only a handful of cages and pens. City voters' rejection of urban renewal in 1958 meant that plans for upgrading the zoo also failed. Zoo leaders were trying to raise funds for a children's zoo in 1963, when Doorly made her gift, stipulating that the zoo be renamed for her husband.[21]

Doorly also said she hoped that animals would be kept in safe settings behind moats and other devices, rather than in "confining cages," to give them as much freedom as possible. After her death, in 1964, her daughter, Kay D. Clark, reinforced her mother's hope "for an open zoo" with a "naturalness of surroundings."[22]

"I visualize that ultimately the zoo will be comparable to some of the zoos which have been established in other cities of comparable or even larger size and will be a truly civic asset to Omaha," she wrote in her donation letter to the Omaha Zoological Society.[23] Gallagher called Doorly's gift "the key that unlocks the city."[24]

Doorly's vision of an open zoo was revolutionary in the 1960s, and it still animates today's world-class Henry Doorly Zoo & Aquarium. Her initiative laid the groundwork for exhibits like today's African Grasslands, where different species share habitat as they would in the wild.

Mary Galligan Cornett: First Lady of City Hall

While Gallagher focused on the parks and Doorly gave Omaha a real zoo, city clerk Mary Galligan Cornett presided over an empire of documents and turned her office into a major power center. Not only was she credited with understanding the intricacies of city government better than anyone; she also helped numerous elected officials master their jobs. As a young reporter, I witnessed one such "class."

After his election in 1973, Mayor Edward Zorinsky removed the door to his office and invited citizens to drop by anytime. I spent a day seeing how this worked. Only a couple of ordinary people stopped by to greet the mayor as he conducted city business. His most impressive caller by far was Cornett, who carried a pile of thick folders into the office and told "Eddie" what to do with each. Sign this, talk to Finance about that, and so on. The novice mayor complied. The session illustrated why Cornett's obituary described her as the "toughminded, politically powerful clerk" and why a former city council member described her as "one of the greatest broads who ever lived," a description friends said she would have loved.[25]

Part of Cornett's power was institutional. Because city clerks have civil service protection, they stay regardless of who is mayor, while elected officials come and go. City clerks understand how city government works because they manage its paperwork, keeping city records, getting contracts signed, and preparing documents for the city council's agenda. "Often the clerk knows that things have been tried and not worked out so they can warn officials," said Cornett's successor Buster Brown. Clerks mostly work behind the scenes.[26]

Cornett understood power because her North Omaha political family had strong ties to city government. Her mother had served on county and state Democratic central committees. She began her fifty-three-year city career in 1945 as a billing clerk while she was a student at the old Omaha University. She learned to operate in the man's world of City Hall, where spittoons were more common than women with clout.[27]

Cornett became city clerk in 1961 and served with fifteen mayors during her thirty-six years in office. "I never saw Mary cave in. I never saw her lose a fight," said former U.S. representative Lee Terry, who served on the city council before being elected to Congress. "She was very protective of city government. That's why she was so protective of the rules."[28]

Brown described Cornett as universally respected and often feared, despite the fact that when someone needed a favor, she would frequently "bend over backwards to help." Visitors to her office would be treated to a lengthy chat about her daughter, Abbie, who became a state senator.[29] Cornett, who got married in 1964 and was widowed during the 1970s, retired in 1997.

She died ten years later from circulatory problems. By her retirement she had been joined by other significant women administrators, including Ruth Jackson, who headed the Human Rights and Relations Department.

Ruth Jackson: Groundbreaking Department Head

Omaha's first woman city department head, Ruth Jackson, of Human Relations, couldn't even get a city secretarial job when she first applied in 1960 because she had supposedly failed a skills test. However, she wasn't allowed to see her score. A few years later she retook the test, this time passing with a high score.

Jackson, an African American, took this as a sign of progress in fighting racial discrimination. She spent the next twenty-one years at City Hall advocating for civil rights in her pleasant but determined fashion. She worked as a secretary under five Human Relations directors before Mayor Al Veys appointed her as director in 1977.[30]

As such, she became the city's face in fighting racism and became known as a color-blind advocate for justice. The Human Rights and Relations Department, as today's department is known, investigates complaints of discrimination. It also oversees compliance with city equal opportunity ordinances, such as those providing opportunities for small and minority businesses to bid on city contracts.[31] Jackson's duties included working to improve housing standards in designated parts of the city.

A native of Omaha who grew up in Clarinda, Iowa, Jackson remained Human Relations Department director under Mayor Mike Boyle until 1985, when she retired because of health problems. She also was active in the Democratic Party and described politics as her favorite sport. She also later served on the City Personnel Board. She died in 1975.[32]

Douglas County Government

It took voters longer to elect women to the Douglas County Board than to the Omaha City Council, but by the early 1990s there were several women county commissioners, including Mary Ann Borgeson, Bernice Labedz, and Carole Woods Harris, the first African American county elected official. Being a groundbreaker was nothing new to Harris, who had spent her life opening doors for minorities and women at Northwestern Bell.

Carole Woods Harris—Groundbreaking County Leader

When Carole Woods Harris graduated with honors from the old Technical High School in the late 1950s, she applied for a job as a long-distance operator with Northwestern Bell. The company rejected her because she was African American but offered her a job as an elevator operator. She refused that position but joined the phone company during the civil rights era, after it offered her the long-distance operator position.

Harris (then named Anders) spent the next thirty years at Bell. She was promoted to district manager for directory publishing, supervising staffs in Omaha, Des Moines, and Minneapolis, then she became Northwestern Bell's director of strategic planning. She gained a reputation for calm competence in working on the transition of Northwestern Bell to U.S. West.[33]

She ran unsuccessfully for city council in 1989 and retired from the phone company in 1990. Two years later she was elected to the county board, Douglas County's first Black elected official.[34] Harris served three terms on the board, focusing on justice issues. She was elected board vice president and then president.

Former city council member Brenda Council, also an African American, said Harris "paved a path that others can follow. . . . Two words that describe her are integrity and dignity. . . . She brings reason and rationality to her decisions. She's just a calm, steady presence."[35]

After leaving the county board, Harris was elected to the State Board of Education. When her term ended, she moved to South Carolina to be closer to family. She has three grown children.[36]

Kathleen Kelley: Top County Administrator

As in city government, modern women have risen to top county administrative jobs. In 1998 Kathleen Kelley became the Douglas County government's first female top administrative executive. She had begun her career as ombudsman in 1989 and became an administrative specialist to the county board before it promoted her to the position that she held until she retired, in 2013.[37]

The Modern Era

Even today, men hold a high percentage of the most important jobs in city government, which are usually drawn from male-dominated fields like engineering, architecture, and finance, said Dr. Carol Ebdon, a public administration professor at UNO, the first, and only, woman to serve as Omaha's finance director.[38]

The longevity of many city department heads also accounts for some of the male dominance, said Dr. Paul Landow, a UNO political science professor and former mayor Mike Fahey's chief of staff. Omaha department heads often serve under several mayors regardless of party affiliation. "You start out with the basic Nebraska nonpartisanship," Landow said. "Most local issues like potholes and trash are traditionally not thought to be partisan." In addition, because the city pays less than private employers, mayors often retain competent administrators who would be difficult to replace. For example, Landow hired Public Works director Robert Stubbe, a top engineer who in 2020 had served three mayors.[39]

In contrast to staff positions, in which there is little turnover, mayors routinely appoint their prominent women supporters to top city advisory boards, such as the Metropolitan Entertainment & Convention Authority (MECA), which governs CHI Health Center and TD Ameritrade Park, according to Landow.[40] Gone are the days when Rachel Gallagher was a rare woman on such unpaid but powerful entities.

For years the city council has had at least one female member, and the growing number of women running for office at all levels makes it likely that there will be more, just as there are in the state legislature and on many elected boards.

14

Civil Rights

Black Omaha's battle for civil rights began early and still continues. Long before there was a civil rights movement, African American women and girls began agitating for change in the schools and in the workplace. *Omaha Star* publisher Mildred Brown started fighting job discrimination during World War II and never stopped. She was one of the founders of the local civil rights movement that paralleled the national movement. African American women and girls marched, protested, litigated, and organized, usually with little acclaim. They were plaintiffs in the lawsuit that desegregated the Omaha Public Schools and scored victories like the recognition of Malcolm X's Omaha birthplace. They also helped build their community from Omaha's early years.

Early Black Omaha Women

The first Black people arrived in Omaha before the Civil War, and by the 1880s's the census recorded about twenty-three hundred Black residents statewide. By 1892, when *Omaha World-Herald* columnist Elia Peattie profiled the community, Omaha was home to about six thousand African Americans.[1] She noted that most Black women did not work outside the home, while men worked in many different jobs—although Omaha had never had a "colored merchant."[2] She recognized the impact of discrimination and applauded the community's progress out of "igno-rance, superstition, fear, [and] servility."[3]

Like white women of the era, African American women were active in churches and clubs. A bicentennial book on notable Nebraska women saluted Lenora Dennis Gray for leading such groups in addition to working in catering, writing poetry and raising eight children. Gray joined the Nebraska Federation of Colored Women's Clubs in 1905 and was active for fifty years. She also helped organize the Eureka Art Club, South Side Civic Club, Mary McLeod Bethune Club, and Civic Matrons Club and was active in the Zion Baptist Church.[4]

In segregated Omaha, African Americans formed their own community within the city. In the late 1940s the community boasted 170 businesses along North Twenty-Fourth Street, and after World War II this tiny, overcrowded area produced some of the nation's best athletes, including Bob Gibson and Gale Sayers.[5] By the 1960s most of Omaha's Black residents were crammed into a two-mile area bounded roughly by Sixteenth, Thirtieth, Cuming, and Ohio Streets, where housing was gen-erally deteriorated and slumlords refused to repair houses built in the 1880s and 1890s.[6]

The area also had its own newspaper, the *Omaha Star*, which Mildred Brown co-founded in 1938 to cover community news that the *Omaha World-Herald* ignored, such as births, deaths, marriages, and civic and social events.

Mildred Brown and the *Omaha Star*

Brown, a native of Bessemer, Alabama, was the nation's only female Black newspaper owner during the 1960s. She and her husband, Shirl Edward Gilbert, came to Omaha from Sioux City, Iowa, in 1937. Originally, she was advertising manager of the *Omaha Guide* newspaper, before the couple launched the *Star*. The paper was successful as a result of Mildred's talent for selling advertising.

When she and Gilbert divorced, in 1943, she resumed using her maiden name, took over the paper, and moved herself and the newspaper office into a converted mortuary, where she lived the rest of her life.[7]

When Brown entered a room, people felt her presence. She always wore vibrantly colored matching suits, shoes, and hats and a corsage. "She was an activist and an amazing person. She had a militant stance . . . and she was unique on top of it all," said Omaha native Cathy Hughes of Washington DC, owner of the nation's largest African American broadcasting company.[8] Hughes's father's accounting office was located in the *Star*'s building.

During World War II Brown urged readers to apply for jobs at the Glenn L. Martin Bomber Plant in Bellevue and advocated ending military segregation. She printed names of employers who discriminated on the front page and encouraged readers to picket local stores that discriminated even though some of them dropped their advertising. Brown also supported sit-ins and protest marches.[9]

The *Star* carried banner headlines covering local civil rights actions such as sit-ins at City Hall, and it hired local civil rights leaders like Charles Washington as reporters. When riots broke out during the 1960s, Brown wrote signed front-page editorials. In 1966 she penned a piece about the demonstrations against racial discrimination in Omaha:

> We cannot commend the methods they used to draw attention to the fact that they were frustrated and despaired because they could not see or feel any appreciable betterment of their lot. Likewise, we cannot commend those who have failed over the past three years to listen to the traditional methods of calling attention to the fact that in Omaha there is discrimination in housing, education, employment and health and welfare services. . . . We think that less atten-

tion should be paid to the methods they used in calling attention to their plight and more to finding some solutions to the causes which brought their actions about.[10]

Rioters burned some North Omaha businesses during the 1966 riot but spared the *Star* because of the community's respect for Brown.

Brown was still running the *Star* when she died unexpectedly, in 1989. She received over 150 awards both before and after her death, including an Unsung Heroine Award from the NAACP in 1981. Omaha's Mildred Brown Strolling Park and Mildred Brown Street honor her memory.[11]

Brown's collaborators in Omaha's early civil rights movement included John Markoe, SJ, a Creighton University Jesuit who started the DePorres Club to combat local racial discrimination. The organization was so controversial that it was not affiliated with the university, even though most of its members were CU students. Brown let them meet in her building and supported them in other ways.

The DePorres Club

The DePorres Club has been described as "ahead of its time" for teaching young Black and white women and men to be grassroots civil rights activists. Markoe, who taught math and philosophy at Creighton, had discovered the oppression of Black people as a seminarian in St. Louis. He and his brother William, also a Jesuit, pledged to work for the salvation of African Americans.[12]

Dennis Holland, a CU student, worked with Markoe to organize the DePorres Club in 1947. Initially, members focused on discrimination within Catholic entities.[13] One of the club's first members was Creighton sophomore Virginia Frederick Walsh. In 1948 the club sent her to Omaha's St. Catherine's Hospital to accuse hospital superior Sister Mary Pauline of discriminating against Black patients. The nun "went ballistic" and simply said no, Walsh recalled years later. "We could have done it better."[14] But Walsh became a lifelong activist, and her mother also joined the club.

For twenty years DePorres Club members battled Jim Crow by sitting in at restaurants, picketing employers who discriminated, petitioning government officials, boycotting businesses that refused to hire Black people for non-menial jobs, and publicizing complaints of racism. In 1948, because of the controversy it created, Creighton quietly forbade it to meet on campus, although Markoe remained its moderator.[15] During the early 1950s the FBI investigated it and other Black activist groups for possible Communist infiltration but found nothing.[16]

Walsh said a majority of DePorres Club members were white but that Black people played important roles, especially Brown. She covered club actions in the *Omaha Star* when the *World-Herald* ignored the group, in addition to providing a meeting space. Sometimes she represented the group in negotiating with employers.[17] Elizabeth Pittman, the first female African American Creighton Law School graduate, assisted with legal matters, and the club backed her successful campaign to become the first African American on the Omaha School Board.[18] Student members Bertha Calloway and Tessie Edwards rose to prominence as adults.

Bertha Calloway participated in various protests, including a sit-in at a restaurant near Creighton in 1948.[19] She spent much of her life hunting through basements and attics to collect artifacts of African American life in Omaha and across Nebraska. In 1962 she founded the Negro Historical Society and in 1976 created the Great Plains Black History Museum. In 2017 the city renamed Lake Street between Twenty-Second and Twenty-Fourth Streets "Bertha Calloway Street." Calloway died later that year.[20] Tessie Edwards converted to Catholicism while she was at Creighton and became one of the first African American teachers in Omaha's Catholic schools after graduating in 1949.[21] She ended her career as a well-known history teacher at Creighton Prep.

Walsh said the DePorres Club helped women overcome their fear of conflict. As members of the club, they had a voice in policy and tactics and learned how to organize their resources to make the world a better place. They also overcame their fear of failing and learned to keep trying. "It was an antidote to the other social messages of submission women received, including a lot of myths about submissive women," Walsh said.[22]

Activism during the 1960s

Rioting and burning in the Near North Side ghetto during the 1960s forced Omaha to confront its long history of racism and the anger of its growing African American population. Between 1960 and 1965 the Black community grew from about thirty thousand to about thirty-five thousand. The newcomers were part of the massive national migration of Black people from the South to the North seeking jobs and a better life. While most settled in North Omaha, some lived in South Omaha near the packinghouses, where many of them worked.[23]

African Americans rebelled against substandard segregated housing, job discrimination, police brutality, and segregated public schools, restaurants, and streetcars. Protests ranged from lobbying, litigation, and peaceful picketing to rioting. Women were among those rebelling. The conditions in the Omaha Public Schools (OPS) were a particular flash point.

Dorothy Eure and the Integration of the Omaha Public Schools

For generations Omaha's public schools were almost as rigidly segregated as those in the South, and conditions in the city's predominately Black schools mirrored those in the southern states, said the Reverend Darryl Eure, pastor of Freestone Baptist Church. African American children were assigned to schools in their segregated neighborhoods, where buildings were inferior to those in white neighborhoods. Children received used textbooks that schools for white children had discarded. Sometimes children in the same classes had different books. There were only a few Black elementary teachers and none in OPS high schools until the late 1950s. Eure's mother, Dorothy, sought to change these conditions. Reverend Eure recalled that his childhood in the 1950s and 1960s revolved around her thirty-year battle to change OPS.[24]

Dorothy Eure began protesting racism while she was a student at Tech High during World War II. She and other Black students formed the Tomorrow's World Club that asked the OPS board to hire Black teachers. At the time, most Black students were assigned to Tech or North High, but children of African American professional families usually attended Central High, which was more academically demanding.

After graduating from Tech, Eure cleaned offices for Ocoma Foods, then cleaned houses and cared for the children of rich white families. "What she did was just like the women in the movie *The Help*," Reverend Eure said.[25]

Later Dorothy Eure got a job cleaning out blood tubes at University Hospital, but by then things were beginning to change, with more opportunities available to people of color. She became a paralegal and joined the Legal Aid Society, specializing in helping people resolve problems with Social Security. Meanwhile, she continued raising her four sons and fighting with OPS. "My mother had been fighting with OPS most of my life," said Reverend Eure, a 1969 graduate of Central High. She also took her sons to protest privately run Peony Park's exclusion of Black people. Her husband, who worked in meatpacking, sometimes half-joked that her activism might cost him his job.[26]

In 1973 Dorothy Eure became one of seven plaintiffs in a successful federal lawsuit challenging segregation in OPS. District administrators blamed school segregation on housing segregation, but the plaintiffs successfully contended that attendance lines were drawn to support segregation. The judge ordered OPS to correct the problem through busing.[27]

Reverend Eure noted that the district quickly improved the North Omaha schools to which whites were bused. For example, the old Horace Mann School became King Science Center, a magnet school with a specialized curriculum and special facilities, including a planetarium.[28] Today OPS uses a variety of methods such as magnet schools to promote voluntary school integration. A street by the old Tech High (today's OPS headquarters) is named in honor of Dorothy Eure and her fellow plaintiff, Lerlean Johnson.

The minister also recalled his mother's Christmas parties for neighborhood children and stressed her concern for everyone in need. "My mother had a great love for people of all races," he said. "She felt that God called her to do this work. She was like a local Mother Teresa." Dorothy Eure died of cancer in 1993.[29] Other prominent local women in the movement included Rowena Moore, who discovered an odd historical connection between her family and Malcolm X.

Rowena Moore's Fight to Honor Malcolm X

By the time that Moore discovered that her family owned the North Omaha lot where the future Malcolm X had lived as a child, she had been fighting racism in packinghouse hiring for years. She admired the civil rights leader and wanted Omaha to honor its tie with him even though he had no love for the city.

In 1926, when Malcolm Little was a small child, white supremacists drove his family out of Omaha. Years later, after that toddler had become Malcolm X, a fiery leader of the Black Muslims, he returned to Omaha to decry its racist past and present.[30] Among his audience in 1964 was Moore, who discovered that her own family owned the property at Thirty-Fourth and Pinckney where

Malcolm's family had lived. Moore launched a campaign to turn it into a national historic site.

Moore had picketed the Armour packinghouse in South Omaha during World War II because it wouldn't hire Black women. She later worked there for twenty years and became a leader of Omaha's integrated packinghouse unions. She later owned a grocery store at Twenty-Eighth and Grant Streets and produced a movie, *The Sacred Beauty*. She was also a Democratic political activist.

Moore's effort to turn the Malcolm X site into a national historic landmark was successful, although she died before the memorial was completed. It was added to the National Register of Historic Places in 1984.[31] Today the Malcolm X House Site in a hilly North Omaha neighborhood is testimony to the power of a determined Black woman.

Other Notable African American Women

Omaha has been home to other notable African American women, including educators and government officials profiled in other chapters. Many of them had to overcome both racial and gender discrimination and battled quietly to open doors for the next generation. Reverend Eure especially saluted Wilda Stephenson, a teacher who was active in the Presbyterian Church and headed UNO's Goodrich Scholarship program, as a major influence on his life. The program aided minority students in graduating from college.[32] Photos of civil rights marches, speeches, and other actions show numerous women whose names are often overlooked but who helped combat racism in their city.

African American women such as Brenda Council, Tanya Cook, and Carole Woods Harris have held local elected office, and Council became the first African American woman to run for mayor. Omaha Public Schools, which at one time would not hire African Americans to teach high school, is now headed by Superintendent Cheryl Logan, an African American.

15

After the Women's Movement

Even though many modern women are impatient with the pace of change in Omaha, it's a different city for women than it was fifty years ago. Doors have opened and glass ceilings fallen in almost every field. One prominent woman who contributed to many of those changes reflected on what she has experienced and helped engender, especially through her key role in creating the Women's Fund of Omaha, which finances services and programs for women and mentors the next generation of female leaders.

From her penthouse home on the top floor of the Woodmen Tower, Dr. Gail Walling Yanney, civic leader and retired physician, can metaphorically look down on the key institutions that shaped her and assess the way that the women's movement has changed this "man's town."

To the north there's all-female Duchesne Academy, where Yanney received a "glorious education" and "met wonderful girls." To the west there's the rapidly expanding University of Nebraska Medical Center (UNMC), where she earned her medical degree in 1961, one of three women in a class of about one hundred. About half of today's classes are female.

Across Farnam Street there's the City-County complex, where Jean Stothert occupies the mayor's office and women judges preside over many courtrooms. Downstairs, in the Woodmen Tower, women routinely earn partnerships at top law firms like Baird Holm. And in an office across the hall from Yanney's home, her daughter, Lisa Roskens, largely manages the successful investment firm founded by her husband, Michael. Both Gail and Michael Yanney have received numerous awards for their service and generosity.

Gail Yanney reflected on how things have changed since she had to get permission from a medical school professor to join the Junior League because they feared the time commitment would interfere with her classes. A doctor who served on the school board granted permission because he liked physicians to be well-rounded.

After graduating from UNMC, Yanney completed a residency in anesthesiology there and entered private practice, in addition to serving as a clinical faculty member at UNMC. She retired in 1986.

As a physician, Yanney worked on a flexible schedule to allow her to spend more time raising Lisa. Now, she notes, most schools offer full-day kindergarten and after-school care programs to meet the needs of mothers with jobs, and she sees "lots of opportunities out there."

"I see a glass half full, but there's still a need for change," she said. "The women's movement has made a difference for women and men. But I worry that we might regress."[1]

Founding the Women's Fund

In 1990 Yanney, who has been active in numerous organizations, played a key role in founding the Women's Fund of Omaha within the Omaha Community Foundation. Since then the fund has raised $35 million for women's programs, in addition to researching and reporting on the needs of women and advocating for policies that benefit women.[2]

Yanney recalled the discussion that led to the fund. "Dale Te Kolste (co-founder of the Community Foundation) took me to lunch and talked about how a great deal of money would be passing generations," Yanney said. Te Kolste, a former top official of Northern Natural Gas, wanted to ensure that women's groups benefited from this wealth.

Yanney, in turn, invited some friends for lunch, and they agreed to seek a $150,000 grant from a joint Ford / MacArthur Fund grant to establish a women's fund. They also raised the required matching money, and "that's how we started." The fund hired Mary Heng-Braun, former executive director of the Girls Club, to run the program, which initially focused on childcare and domestic violence. It also made modest grants to women's organizations.[3] Since then it has continued to grow and has become a major force for women in Omaha.

The Women's Fund Today

Thirty years after its founding, the Women's Fund of Omaha still receives no public money. It focuses on four major areas, according to its former executive director, Michelle Zych: freedom from violence, including efforts to combat domestic violence, sexual assault, and sex trafficking; economic security, including work for paid family leave, pay equity, and combating payday lending; leadership development through circles that promote mentoring and connections among women at various stages of their careers; access to sexual and reproductive health care, including supporting clinics around Nebraska that provide free testing for sexually transmitted diseases and contraception for women aged fifteen to twenty-four.[4]

Like Yanney, Zych said she sees progress for women, but she's not satisfied. "I would have thought we would be further. Now we have to shift and adjust and move forward."[5] Zych said she's pleased that both Omaha's mayor and the superintendent of the Omaha Public Schools are women, but she is concerned that there are still too few women in leadership roles. Currently she is helping more women become community leaders, especially women of color, who are often excluded from leadership opportunities. "We have to make sure there is room at the table for them so that more women can bring their different perspectives to the table," she said. This is especially important as Omaha becomes a more diverse city and more of its future leaders are women and men from a variety of racial and cultural backgrounds, instead of mostly white men. In 2021 Jo Giles, an African American strategic communicator and community activist, was named executive director of the Women's Fund.

It is interesting to note that the Women's Fund plays a role similar to that of the Mayor's Commission on the Status of Women in the 1970s, serving as a catalyst for change. However, because it is privately funded and governed, unlike the commission, it cannot be disbanded for displeasing elected officials. And young women are stepping up to lead women's empowerment into the future.

Retrospect on the Future

On a winter evening in 2020, a diverse group of about thirty women, mostly millennials who had come directly from their jobs, assembled at Spezia Restaurant for beverages, snacks, and an update on the Women's Fund's activities in the Nebraska Unicameral. The fund's lobbyist described a half-dozen bills it was supporting, dealing with issues such as services to rape victims and opposition to payday lending. Women senators sponsored many of the bills.

The women in this book would be so excited by that evening at Spezia. The suffragists would cheer to learn about women senators pushing women's issues—clear evidence that their sacrifices were worth it. Josie Washburn would be delighted that the Women's Fund advocates for victims of sex trafficking, just as she exposed the evils of prostitution. Betty Abbott, Mary Cornett, and Rachel Gallagher would marvel at the number of women in pol-

itics. The doors they opened will not close. The pioneer teachers would be proud of their successors for preparing this group
of confident young female leaders.

So, to return to the central questions of this book, is Omaha
really a man's town? Has it ever been? Or have many Omahans
just failed to acknowledge the contributions of women, past and
present, who have played consequential roles in building today's
city—and also failed to imagine women's lives in the city's future?

Consider the women in this book and answer these questions.
Will today's young women see as many changes in their daughters' lives as their mothers do in theirs?

Acknowledgments

No one writes a book without help from many people, more than can be recognized. However, I extend special thanks to these people who played important roles in bringing this book to life.

I am especially indebted to Bridget Barry, acquisitions editor for the University of Nebraska Press. She guided me through organizing the text and provided the constructively critical feedback without which there would be no book. Thank you!

No one should ever write a book on Omaha history without the assistance of the Local History staff of the Omaha Public Library. Special thanks to Martha Grenzeback and Lynn Sullivan, who suggested numerous references and patiently answered my many questions. They are the best.

David Bristow, editor the *Nebraska History Magazine* for History Nebraska, was extremely helpful whenever I sought his assistance on articles or historic photographs.

Special thanks also to my close friend Carol McCabe, who assisted me with the photos for this book and, along with former Creighton archivist David Crawford, provided numerous photographs.

Thanks to all interviewees who shared their own stories or their insights of their family members. Their names are listed in the bibliography.

I particularly want to thank the people who helped identify women who should be discussed in the various chapters or provided background on historical events and groups of women or other aid. They include Dr. Audrey Paulman; Professor Emeritus Richard Shugrue; Lyn Wallin Ziegenbein; Connie Spellman; Mary Heng-Braun; Barbara Haggart; James Fogarty; Joan Fogarty; Elizabeth Rea; Barry Combs; Dr. Keith Bigsby; John Krecek; Tami Buffalohead-McGill; Mary Maxwell; Vivian Amu; Dr. Carol Ebdon; Michael Mclarney; Margo Bieker; Sister Susan Severin, RSM; Melissa Farris; Monte Kniffen; Josh Bucy; and Ellie Batt.

Thanks to Dr. Heather Fryer of the Creighton History Department for referring two excellent student research assistants, Ann-Clair MacArt and Grace Boothe, who checked and formatted citations. And to Emily Rust for helping with digitizing the manuscript.

I also am indebted to my close friends who supported me during this process, including Jeanne Weeks; Liz Sundem; my sister, Dr. Jan Poley; Mary Heng-Braun; Merrilee Miller; Phyllis Choat; the late Jane O'Brien; my cousin Marylou Garrett; and others such as my "Wine and Whine" group and the gang at Legacy Preservation.

I have dedicated this book to my biggest cheerleader, my daughter, Shanti Psota, and to all the students, especially the women, I was privileged to teach at Creighton University. My goal in writing women's history is to inspire the young women of the future.

Notes

Preface

1. Federal Writers' Project, *Omaha Guide to City and County*, 31.

Introduction

1. Bristow, *Dirty Wicked Town*, 83–92.
2. Carey, *Romance of Omaha*, 47.
3. Bristow, *Dirty Wicked Town*, 3–4.
4. Bristow, *Dirty Wicked Town*, 3–4.
5. Sorenson, *Story of Omaha*, 58–60.
6. Bristow, *Dirty Wicked Town*, 17–18.
7. Sorenson, *Story of Omaha*, 225.
8. Bristow, *Dirty Wicked Town*, 18–19.
9. Bristow, *Dirty Wicked Town*, 20.
10. Sorenson, *Story of Omaha*, 89.
11. Burkley, *Faded Frontier*, 365.
12. Wirth and McCabe, *Omaha's Historic Houses of Worship*, 15.
13. Wirth and McCabe, *Omaha's Historic Houses of Worship*, 15.
14. Sorenson, *Story of Omaha*, 195–96.
15. Sorenson, *Story of Omaha*, 63.
16. Sorenson, *Story of Omaha*, 240.
17. Dustin, *Omaha and Douglas County*, 54.
18. Carey, *Romance of Omaha*, 11.
19. Broadfield, *Stories of Omaha*, 105.

1. Education

1. Rea, *Omaha / Douglas County History Timeline*, 26.
2. Combs and Wigton, *Central High School Historical Timeline*, 6.
3. Combs and Wigton, *Central High School*, 7.

4. Combs and Wigton, *Central High School*, 8.

5. Reese, *Origins of the American High School*, 179.

6. Bigsby, Keith, retired principal, Central High School, interview by author, May 16, 2018.

7. Combs and Wigton, *Central High School*, 10.

8. Bigsby interview.

9. Bigsby interview.

10. Combs and Wigton, *Central High School*, 8.

11. Combs and Wigton, *Central High School*, 11.

12. Combs and Wigton, *Central High School*, 17.

13. Combs and Wigton, *Central High School*, 18.

14. "First Woman Principal of the Omaha High School," *Omaha World-Herald*, June 25, 1911, 34.

15. "Forty Years as a Teacher, Omaha Women to Retire in Her Prime," *Omaha World-Herald*, January 25, 1914, 35.

16. Bigsby interview.

17. "Kate McHugh: Distinguished Faculty," Central High School Foundation, accessed November 11, 2019, https://chsfomaha.org/events/hall-of-fame?id=60.

18. Ralph Sweeley, "For a Kate McHugh School," Public Pulse, *Omaha World-Herald*, April 3, 1972, 20.

19. "Forty Years as a Teacher."

20. "Kate McHugh."

21. "Fifty Years Ago," *Omaha World-Herald*, March 11, 1914, 59.

22. "Omaha Diary for December 16, 1911," *Omaha World-Herald*, December 16, 1936, 5.

23. "Declares That Jobs Big Negro Problem," *Omaha World-Herald*, September 29, 1931, 3.

24. "Forty Years Ago," *Omaha World-Herald*, June 5, 1959, 14.

25. Scott Wilson, history teacher, Central High School, interview by author, November 11, 2019.

26. "Memorial to Miss McHugh," *Omaha World-Herald*, June 18, 1931, 23.

27. Joan Fogarty, Omaha historian and former staffer, Benson High School, interview by author, January 21, 2019.

28. Fogarty interview.

29. "Lucinda Williams," North Omaha History, accessed July 6, 2020, https://northomahahistory.com.

30. Betsie Freeman, "Longtime Omaha Educator Katherine Fletcher, 96, Was 'Very Ladylike but Fun-Loving,'" *Omaha World-Herald*, April 10, 2014.

31. Girls Incorporated of Omaha, "Girls Inc. Breaks Ground on 55,000 Square Foot Facility Expansion," Girls Inc. Omaha News, June 1, 2014, https://girlsincomaha.org/girls-inc-breaks-ground-on-55000-square-foot-facility-expansion.

32. "Here's a Possible New Name for Burke High," Omaha.com, June 29, 2020.

33. Erin Duffy, Omaha.com, October 16, 2019.

34. Omaha Public Schools, accessed September 20, 2020, https://district.ops.org.

35. "Dr. Cheryl Logan Began Her Position as Superintendent of Omaha Public Schools on July 1, 2018," Omaha Public School District website, accessed November 11, 2019, https://district.ops.org/DEPARTMENTS/OfficeoftheSuperintendent.aspx.

36. "Here's a Possible New Name for Burke High."

37. "History of Catholic Education in the United States," Wikipedia, accessed September 20, 2020, https://en.wikipedia.org/wiki/History_of_Catholic_education_in_the_United_States.

38. Susan Severin, RSM, archivist, Sisters of Mercy, interview by author, January 8, 2019.

39. Severin interview.

40. Muldrey, *Abounding in Mercy*, 70–72.

41. O'Brien, *Journeys*, 72.

42. O'Brien, *Journeys*, 74.

43. O'Brien, *Journeys*, 74–75.

44. Severin interview.

45. Muldrey, *Abounding in Mercy*, 75.

46. Muldrey, *Abounding in Mercy*, 80.

47. Carey, *Romance of Omaha*, 72.

48. David Peters, head of school, Mount Michael Benedictine School, interview by author, January 21, 2019.

49. Brownell-Talbot School, "Brownell-Talbot School History," accessed February 12, 2019, www.brownell.edu/about-bt/history.

50. Clark Potter, "Historical Sketch," 52–53.

51. Clark Potter, "Historical Sketch," 76.

52. Clark Potter, "Historical Sketch," 66.

53. Clark Potter, "Historical Sketch," 92.

54. Brownell-Talbot School, "Brownell-Talbot School History."

55. Brownell-Talbot School, "Brownell-Talbot School History."

56. Audrey Kauders, retired executive, Joslyn Art Museum, interview by author, February 9, 2019.

57. Clark Potter, "Historical Sketch," 22.

2. Creighton and Duchesne

1. Dennis Mihelich, retired professor of history, Creighton University, interview by author, November 27, 2018.

2. Mihelich interview.

3. Ann McGill, Creighton family descendant, interview by author, December 11, 2018.

4. Mihelich, *History of Creighton*, ix.

5. Mihelich, *History of Creighton*, 22.

6. Mihelich, *History of Creighton*, 9.

7. Mihelich, *History of Creighton*, 27.

8. Mary Maxwell, Creighton family descendant and public speaker, interview by author, November 28, 2018.

9. Maxwell interview.

10. Mihelich, *History of Creighton*, 26.

11. Mihelich, *History of Creighton*, 33–35.

12. Mihelich, *History of Creighton*, 29.

13. Mihelich, *History of Creighton*, 39.

14. Mihelich, *History of Creighton*, 43.

15. Mihelich, *History of Creighton*, 34.

16. Mihelich, *History of Creighton*, 64.

17. Mihelich, *History of Creighton*, 44.

18. Mihelich, *History of Creighton*, 62.

19. Mihelich, *History of Creighton*, 28.

20. Mihelich, *History of Creighton*, 28.

21. Mary Monson, retired history teacher, Duchesne Academy, interview by author, December 19, 2018.

22. Margo Bieker, volunteer activist, Duchesne Academy, interview by author, July 8, 2018.

23. *Duchesne*, 2–3.

24. Quest, *Duchesne College & Academy*, 1.

25. Callan, *Society of the Sacred Heart*, 681–82.

26. Callan, *Society of the Sacred Heart*, 684.

27. Monson interview.

28. Callan, *Society of the Sacred Heart*, 684.

29. *Duchesne*, 10.

30. Mihelich, *History of Creighton*, 118.

3. Native American Women

1. Starita, *Warrior*, 47–48.

2. Starita, *Warrior*, 12–13.

3. Giffen, with LaFlesche, *Oo-Mah-Ha Ta-Wa-Tha*, 30–34.

4. Starita, *Warrior*, 30–37.

5. Starita, *Warrior*, 43–44.

6. Starita, *Warrior*, 4–5.

7. Starita, *Warrior*, 113.

8. Starita, *Warrior*, 53–54.

9. Starita, *Warrior*, 55–56.

10. Starita, *Warrior*, 62.

11. Starita, *Warrior*, 63.

12. Starita, *Warrior*, 64.

13. Carolyn Johnson, descendant of Bright Eyes LaFlesche, interview by author, April 18, 2019.

14. Starita, *Warrior*, 65.

15. Starita, *Warrior*, 66.

16. Starita, *Warrior*, 170–72.

17. John Krecek, retired Creighton University registrar, interview by author, June 10, 2020.

18. Krecek interview.

19. Haynes, *History of the Trans-Mississippi*, 220.

20. Krecek interview.

21. Haynes, *History of the Trans-Mississippi*, 231.

22. Margucrite Johnson, descendant of Bright Eyes LaFlesche, interview by author, April 18, 2019.

23. Starita, *Warrior*, 217–18.

24. C. Johnson interview; M. Johnson interview.

25. Rudi Mitchell, PhD, former chairman of the Omaha Tribe, interview by author, June 18, 2020.

Interlude 1. "New Women" of the Gilded Age

1. Bloomfield, *Impertinences*, 162–63.

2. Sorenson, *Story of Omaha*, 612–13.

3. Wheeler, *Almanac of Nebraska*, 128–29.

4. Pollak, *Welcome to Omaha*, 114–15.

5. Wirth, *From Society Page to Front Page*, 31.

6. Pratt, "'Union Maids,'" 197–99.

7. Tyler and Auerbach, *History of Medicine*, 179–81.

8. Lynn Sullivan, local historian, Omaha Public Library, interview by author, June 25, 2018.

9. Wirth, *From Society Page to Front Page*, 19.

10. Wirth, "Heckling the President," 53.

4. Votes for Omaha Women

1. Wilhite, "Sixty-Five Years," 150.

2. Wilhite, "Sixty-Five Years," 150.

3. Wilhite, "Sixty-Five Years," 150.

4. Collins, *America's Women*, 113–14.

5. Collins, *America's Women*, 319.

6. Gattey, *Bloomer Girls*, 36–37.

7. Gattey, *Bloomer Girls*, 134.

8. Wilhite, "Sixty-Five Years," 149.

9. Wilhite, "Sixty-Five Years," 169.

10. Wilhite, "Sixty-Five Years," 151.

11. Wilhite, "Sixty-Five Years," 152.

12. Wilhite, "Sixty-Five Years," 152.

13. Wilhite, "Sixty-Five Years," 152.

14. Wilhite, "Sixty-Five Years," 151.

15. *Votes for Women: Nebraska's Suffrage Story*, exhibit, History Nebraska, Lincoln: Nebraska State Museum, 2019.

16. Rea, *Omaha / Douglas County History Timeline*, 37.

17. Governor's Commission on the Status of Women, *Nebraska Women*, 24.

18. *Votes for Women*, exhibit.

19. Hickman, "Thou Shalt Not Vote," 55–56.

20. Hickman, "Anti-Suffrage in Nebraska," 60.

21. Hickman, "Anti-Suffrage in Nebraska," 61.

22. Hickman, "Anti-Suffrage in Nebraska," 58.

23. Hickman, "Anti-Suffrage in Nebraska," 59.

24. Pratt, "'Union Maids,'" 200.

25. Rea, *Omaha / Douglas County History Timeline*, 72.

26. *Votes for Women*, exhibit.

27. Hickman, "Anti-Suffrage in Nebraska," 55.

28. Wirth, "Heckling the President," 50.

29. Wirth, "Heckling President Wilson," 50.

30. Wirth, "Heckling President Wilson," 52.

31. Wirth, "Heckling President Wilson," 53.

32. Sally Bisson-Best, "Doris Stevens: Nebraska's Forgotten Suffrage Leader," in *Votes for Women*, 54–59.

33. Hickman, "Anti-Suffrage in Nebraska," 55.

34. Bristow, "Mabel Gillespie."

5. Prostitution in Wide-Open Omaha

1. Bristow, *Dirty Wicked Town*, 201.

2. U.S. Census (1910).

3. Bristow, *Dirty Wicked Town*, 208.

4. Jane Palmer, "Omaha's Hidden History," *Omaha World-Herald*, August 3, 2006, 10.

5. Bristow, *Dirty Wicked Town*, 202.

6. Menard, *Political Bossism*, 206–7.

7. Menard, *Political Bossism*, 206–7.

8. Bristow, *Dirty Wicked Town*, 204.

9. Bristow, *Dirty Wicked Town*, 203.

10. Bristow, *Dirty Wicked Town*, 203.

11. Bristow, *Dirty Wicked Town*, 205.

12. Collins, *America's Women*, 112.

13. Menard, *Political Bossism*, 207.

14. Menard, *Political Bossism*, 207.

15. Sorenson, *Story of Omaha*, 474.

16. Bristow, *Dirty Wicked Town*, 209.

17. Hoctor, "Case of the Mysterious Magnanimous Madam," 2.

18. James D. Fogarty, "A Tribute to Anna Wilson," presentation, May 30, 2016.

19. Hoctor, "Case of the Mysterious Magnanimous Madam," 6.

20. Bristow, *Dirty Wicked Town*, 210–11.

21. Bristow, *Dirty Wicked Town*, 210–11.

22. Fogarty, "Tribute."

23. Bristow, *Dirty Wicked Town*, 211.

24. Fogarty, "Tribute."

25. "Anna Wilson Offers Hospital to City; More Gifts Intimated," *Omaha Daily News*, August 2, 1911, 1.

26. Fogarty, "Tribute."

27. Fogarty, "Tribute."

28. Fogarty, "Tribute."

29. Bristow, *Dirty Wicked Town*, 199–200.

30. Bristow, *Dirty Wicked Town*, 199.

31. Bristow, *Dirty Wicked Town*, 200.

32. Bristow, *Dirty Wicked Town*, 209.

33. Enns, "Wild Women Wednesday."

34. Menard, *Political Bossism*, 209.

35. Bristow, *Dirty Wicked Town*, 207.

36. Menard, *Political Bossism*, 207–10.

37. Menard, *Political Bossism*, 211.

38. Bristow, *Dirty Wicked Town*, 206.

39. Bristow, *Dirty Wicked Town*, 207.

40. Bloomfield, *Impertinences*, 80.

41. Bloomfield, *Impertinences*, 81.

42. Julie Cornell, "Cash Offered to Turn in Sex Traffickers," KETV News, August 18, 2021, https://www.ketv.com/article/they-are-abused-physically-mentally-spiritually/37311615.

6. Health Care

1. Bloomfield, *Impertinences*, 162–63.

2. Bloomfield, *Impertinences*, 53–58.

3. Lenhoff, *History of Bishop Clarkson Memorial Hospital*, 1.

4. Lenhoff, *History of Bishop Clarkson Memorial Hospital*, 1.

5. "130 Years & Going Strong," 11.

6. Dustin, *Omaha and Douglas County*, 182.

7. Dustin, *Omaha and Douglas County*, 182.

8. Mihelich, *History of Creighton*, 73.

9. Mihelich, *History of Creighton*, 73.

10. Mihelich, *History of Creighton*, 73.

11. Mihelich, *History of Creighton*, 172.

12. Sasse, "History of North Omaha's Immanuel Hospital."

13. Mihelich, *History of Creighton*, 173.

14. Julia McCord, "Creighton Professor Honored in Europe," *Omaha World-Herald*, December 16, 2001, 7B.

15. Barbara Braden, retired dean and nursing professor, Creighton University, interview by author, February 28, 2019.

16. Burbach, "Dr. Rena Boyle."

17. Burbach, "Dr. Rena Boyle."

18. "Patach, Dorothy," Omaha.com, February 23, 2019, www.omaha.com/obits.

19. "Patach, Dorothy," Omaha.com.

20. Braden interview.

21. Braden interview.

22. Tyler, and Auerbach, *History of Medicine*, 174.

23. Tyler and Auerbach, *History of Medicine*, 181.

24. Tyler and Auerbach, *History of Medicine*, 179–81.

25. "Methodist Memories: Dr. Mary J. Breckenridge (1839–1924)," Employee Connections, May 16, 2016, http://www.mhsec.com/news/1260.

26. Andrews-Koryta, "Dr. Olga Stastny," 20–21.

27. Andrews-Koryta, "Dr. Olga Stastny," 20–23.

28. Andrews-Koryta, "Dr. Olga Stastny," 24.

29. Andrews-Koryta, "Dr. Olga Stastny," 25.

30. Andrews-Koryta, "Dr. Olga Stastny," 26.

31. Paulman and Schlelcher, "History of Omaha's Unrivaled Facilities," 15.

32. "Condon, Surgeon, Native of Indianapolis, Is Dead," *Indianapolis Star*, May 28, 1939, 7.

33. "Mrs. Lillian Condon Dies at Hospital," *Omaha World-Herald*, August 7, 1940, 6.

34. "Muriel R. Frank," 24–25.

35. "Muriel R. Frank," 24.

36. James Steinberg, physician and son of Dr. Muriel Frank, interview by author, February 23, 2019.

37. Steinberg interview.

38. Steinberg interview.

39. "Muriel R. Frank," 24.

40. Steinberg interview.

7. Human Services

1. Michael Mclarney, former director, United Way of the Midlands, interview by author, April 23, 2019.

2. Carey, *Romance of Omaha*, 72.

3. Bloomfield, *Impertinences*, 32.

4. Bloomfield, *Impertinences*, 67.

5. Bloomfield, *Impertinences*, 37.

6. Bloomfield, *Impertinences*, 67.

7. Bloomfield, *Impertinences*, 43.

8. Bloomfield, *Impertinences*, 49.

9. Bloomfield, *Impertinences*, 51.

10. Pollak, *Welcome to Omaha*, 104–5.

11. Julia McCord, "Christ Child Center Director Mary Flannigan Dies at Age 85," *Omaha World-Herald*, February 6, 2003, 4B.

12. Cindy Gonzalez, "One Year Stretches to 43 for Christ Child Director," *Omaha World-Herald*, June 13, 1986.

13. McCord, "Christ Child Center Director."

14. Cindy Gonzalez, "Christ Child to Close Main Center in Little Italy," Omaha.com, August 14, 2015.

15. Cindy Gonzalez, "Without Longtime Home, Christ Child Society Uses Pop-Ups to Help Families," Omaha.com, October 21, 2019.

16. Oursler and Oursler, *Father Flanagan*, 203.

17. Thomas Lynch, director, Boys Town Museum, interview by author, May 2, 2019.

18. Oursler and Oursler, *Father Flanagan*, 148.

19. Oursler and Oursler, *Father Flanagan*, 100.

20. Oursler and Oursler, *Father Flanagan*, 148.

21. Lynch interview.

22. Lynch interview.

23. Lynch and Hyland, *Boys Town Story*, 32; Lynch interview.

24. Lynch and Hyland, *Boys Town Story*, 22–23.

25. Lynch interview.

26. Lynch and Hyland, *Boys Town Story*, 44–45.

27. Lynch and Hyland, *Boys Town Story*, 68.

28. Lynch and Hyland, *Boys Town Story*, 95.

29. Barbara Haggart, retired executive, Greater Omaha Chamber of Commerce, and leader of Junior League of Omaha, interview by author May 20, 2019.

30. Mclarney interview.

31. Haggart interview.

32. Haggart interview.

33. Mclarney interview.

34. Haggart interview.

35. Mclarney interview.

36. "Women Cite Agency Disparities," *Omaha World-Herald*, August 17, 1976, 4.

37. Polk, *Black Men and Women*, 55.

38. Polk, *Black Men and Women*, 55.

39. Marian Andersen, Omaha philanthropist and civic leader, interview by author, April 15, 2019.

40. Andersen interview.

41. Andersen interview.

42. Haggart interview.

43. Mclarney interview.

8. Culture and the Arts

1. Katz, *Trans-Mississippi and International Expositions*, 210–12.
2. Katz, *Trans-Mississippi and International Expositions*, 216–17.
3. Katz, *Trans-Mississippi and International Expositions*, 224.
4. Katz, *Trans-Mississippi and International Expositions*, 117.
5. Kiper, *Joslyns of Lynhurst*, 115.
6. Rea, *Omaha / Douglas County History*, 18.
7. Rea, *Omaha / Douglas County History*, 25.
8. Rea, *Omaha / Douglas County History*, 36.
9. Sorenson, *Story of Omaha*, 248–49.
10. Kiper, *Joslyns*, 115.
11. Kalisch, "Early History of the Omaha Public Library," 19, 28.
12. Kiper, *Joslyns*, 115.
13. Haynes, *History of the Trans-Mississippi*, 236.
14. Haynes, *History of the Trans-Mississippi*, 310.
15. Katz, *Trans-Mississippi and International Expositions*, 115.
16. Haynes, *History of the Trans-Mississippi*, 140, 237.
17. Katz, *Trans-Mississippi and International Expositions*, 116.
18. Haynes, *History of the Trans-Mississippi*, 313–14.
19. Kiper, *Joslyns*, 6–7.
20. Penelope Smith, former archivist, Joslyn Castle, interview by author, December 17, 2018.
21. "About: The Castle," Joslyn Castle.com, accessed January 8, 2018, https://joslyncastle.com/about/the-castle.html.
22. Smith interview.
23. Kiper, *Joslyns*, 108.
24. Kiper, *Joslyns*, 115–16.
25. Kiper, *Joslyns*, 116.
26. Kiper, *Joslyns*, 117.
27. Kiper, *Joslyns*, 116.
28. Kiper, *Joslyns*, 117.
29. Kiper, *Joslyns*, 117.
30. "Mrs. Joslyn to Build Memorial," *Sunday World-Herald*, May 6, 1928, 1.
31. "Mrs. Joslyn's Gift," *Morning World-Herald*, May 7, 1928, 1.
32. Kiper, *Joslyns*, 119.
33. "Nebraska's Largest Art Museum," Joslyn.org, accessed January 6, 2018, https://www.joslyn.org/about/history.
34. Kiper, *Joslyns*, 120.
35. Rea, *Omaha / Douglas County History*, 83.
36. Rea, *Omaha / Douglas County History*, 83–84.
37. Jeanne Salerno, former president, the Junior League of Omaha, interview by author, February 5, 2019.

38. Junior League of Omaha, "Historical Summary," 36.

39. Lonnie Pierson Dunbier, *Their Place, Their Time*, 3.

40. Charles Gifford, Omaha architect and son of Emmy Gifford, interview by author, February 8, 2019.

41. Audrey Kauders, retired executive, Joslyn Art Museum, and former director of the Museum of Nebraska Art, interview by author, February 9, 2019.

42. Gifford interview.

43. Elizabeth Flynn, "Spotlight Turns on Godmother Gifford's Backstage Talent," *Omaha World-Herald*, March 26, 1978, 85.

44. Flynn, "Spotlight Turns," 85.

45. Gifford interview.

46. Dunbier, *Their Place, Their Time*, 4.

47. Gifford interview.

48. Kauders interview.

49. Dunbier, *Their Place, Their Time*, 4.

50. Dunbier, *Their Place, Their Time*, 4.

51. Kauders interview.

52. "Ree Kaneko," People Pill, accessed December 10, 2019, http://peoplepill.com /people/ree-kaneko.

53. Bemis Center for Contemporary Arts, accessed December 10, 2019, https:// bemiscenter.org.

54. Leo Biga, "Chamber Honors," *Metro Magazine*, April 2012.

55. Kauders interview.

Interlude 2. World War I to World War II

1. Larsen and Cottrell, *Gate City*, 156.

2. Larsen and Cottrell, *Gate City*, 168.

3. Larsen and Cottrell, *Gate* City, 170–71.

4. Larsen and Cottrell, *Gate City*, 172–73.

5. Andrea Kszystyniak, "Prohibition and Nebraska: In a Largely Dry State, Omaha Wanted Alcohol 'Cheap and Available,'" *Omaha World-Herald*, Go Newsletter, April 9, 2017, 1–3.

6. Kszystyniak, "Prohibition and Nebraska," 1–3.

7. Wirth, *From Society Page to Front Page*, 68.

8. Kszystyniak, "Prohibition and Nebraska," 1–3.

9. Rea, *Omaha / Douglas County History Timeline*.

10. Rea, *Omaha / Douglas County History Timeline*.

11. Wirth, *From Society Page to Front Page*, 79–82.

12. Larsen and Cottrell, *Gate City*.

13. Wirth, *From Society Page to Front Page*, 77–78.

14. Rea, *Omaha / Douglas County History Timeline*.

9. Business

1. Dan McCann, "Who's Who in the Omaha Business Hall of Fame," Omaha.com, April 8, 2018.

2. Lyn Wallin Ziegenbein, retired executive director, Peter Kiewit Foundation, interview by author, June 4, 2019.

3. Limprecht, *Kiewit Story*, 18, 104.

4. Ziegenbein interview.

5. Brad Ashford, former Nebraska congressman and state senator, interview by author, June 11, 2019.

6. Ashford interview.

7. Ashford interview.

8. Ashford interview.

9. Ashford interview.

10. Martin Shukert, principal, RDG Shukert, and former Omaha planning director, interview by author, June 14, 2019.

11. Shukert interview.

12. Shukert interview.

13. Susan Szalewski, "Doris Shukert, 85, Made Time for Others," *Omaha World-Herald*, March 19, 2007, 4B.

14. Women's Fund of Omaha, "Women in Leadership 2016 Executive Summary," accessed June 19, 2019, https://www.omahawomensfund.org/wp-content/uploads/2016-Women-In-Leadership_Executive-Summary_SCREEN-FRIENDLY.pdf.

15. Joni Eliff, "Mrs. Criss History," speech, March 2019.

16. "Builder of Mutual, Mrs. Criss, Dies," *Omaha World-Herald*, March 20, 1978.

17. Elaine Allen, administrator, Mutual of Omaha, interview by author, September 24, 2019.

18. Eliff speech.

19. Allen interview.

20. "Builder of Mutual."

21. Eliff speech.

22. Janice Stoney, retired CEO, Northwestern Bell Telephone Co., interview by author, June 8, 2019.

23. Stoney interview.

24. Stoney interview.

25. Stoney interview.

26. Stoney interview.

27. Robert Dorr, "Rose Blumkin, 1893–1998, Remembering Mrs. B. Hallmark of Legendary Retailer's Life: Honesty," *Omaha World-Herald*, August 10, 1998, 1.

28. Dorr, "Rose Blumkin."

29. Dorr, "Rose Blumkin."

30. Dorr, "Rose Blumkin."

31. Dorr, "Rose Blumkin."
32. Dorr, "Rose Blumkin."
33. Dorr, "Rose Blumkin."
34. Dorr, "Rose Blumkin."
35. Dorr, "Rose Blumkin."
36. Connie Spellman, retired director of Omaha by Design, interview by author, December 20, 2019.
37. Spellman interview.
38. Spellman interview.

10. Restaurants and Bakeries

1. Reiner, *Lost Restaurants*, 71–73.
2. Reiner, *Lost Restaurants*, 75–76.
3. Jim Trebbien, retired dean, Metropolitan Community College Culinary Arts Program, interview by author, August 12, 2019.
4. Trebbien interview.
5. Reine, *Lost Restaurants*, 64–69.
6. Junior League of Omaha, *Toast to Omaha*, 134.
7. Reine, *Lost Restaurants*, 42–54.
8. Jack Kawa, retired owner of Johnny's Café, interview by author, September 18, 2019.
9. Biga, "Charles Hall's Fair Deal Café."
10. Andrew Nelson, "Patricia 'Big Mama' Barron, 76—Soul Food Was North O Restauranteur's Forte," *Omaha World-Herald*, March 31, 2018, 6B.
11. Patricia Sindelar, "M's Pub Founder Mary Vogel Dies," *Omaha World-Herald*, August 14, 2000, 12.
12. Sarah Baker Hansen, "M's Pub Had That Rarest of Restaurant Qualities: Everybody Liked It," *Omaha World-Herald*, January 15, 2016.
13. Sindelar, "M's Pub."
14. Omaha Hospitality Hall of Fame, "Ann Mellen," accessed September 18, 2019, https://omahahospitalityhalloffame.com.
15. Erin Grace, "Gerda Had Grit, a Huge Heart," *Omaha World-Herald*, June 22, 2018.

11. Sports

1. Lindell, "'Nebraska Cyclone,'" 198.
2. Lindell, "'Nebraska Cyclone,'" 201.
3. Lindell, "'Nebraska Cyclone,'" 201.
4. Lindell, "'Nebraska Cyclone,'" 196.
5. Macy, *Wheels of Change*, back cover.
6. Lindell, "'Nebraska Cyclone,'" 198.
7. Lindell, "'Nebraska Cyclone,'" 202.
8. Lindell, "'Nebraska Cyclone,'" 203.

9. Lindell, "'Nebraska Cyclone,'" 205.

10. Benjamin Rader, retired professor of history, University of Nebraska–Lincoln, interview by author, July 11, 2019.

11. Goldblatt, *Games*, 78.

12. Goldblatt, *Games*, 170.

13. "Mabel Lee: The Woman," *Nebraska U: A Collaborative History*, 1, accessed July 29, 2019, https://unlhistory.unl.edu/exhibits/show/lee-pound/mabel-lee--the-woman.

14. "Mabel Lee," 2.

15. "Mabel Lee," 2.

16. "Mabel Lee," 2.

17. Jann and Lawrence "Red" Thomas, outstanding golfer and civic leaders, interview by author, August 1, 2019.

18. Jann and Lawrence Thomas interview.

19. Jann and Lawrence Thomas interview.

20. Jann and Lawrence Thomas interview.

21. Mary Higgins, president, Marian High School, and former women's coach, Creighton University, interview by author, July 23, 2019.

22. Connie Claussen, former head of women's athletics, University of Nebraska at Omaha, interview by author, July 15, 2019.

23. Claussen interview.

24. Claussen interview.

25. Claussen interview.

26. Tony Boone, "Connie Claussen Started Women's Athletics at UNO," Omaha.com, June 9, 2019, 2, https://omaha.com/sports/college/uno/connie-claussen-started-womens -athletics-at-uno-now-a-new-stadium-fulfills-another-dream/article_d9865fbf-8534-59a0 -aa85-fdd7ca30a9b7.html.

27. Higgins interview.

28. Higgins interview.

29. Higgins interview.

30. Higgins interview.

31. Debra Velder, retired executive, Nebraska School Activities Association, interview by author, August 1, 2019.

32. Velder interview.

33. Velder interview.

34. Sullivan, *Nebraska 100*.

Interlude 3. Postwar to the Women's Movement

1. Larsen and Cottrell, *Gate City*, 350.

2. U.S. Census (1970).

3. Larsen and Cottrell, *Gate City*, 291.

12. Law

1. Richard Shugrue, retired professor of law, Creighton University, interview by author, February 18, 2019.

2. "A Mighty Trial Lives On after 50 Years," *Omaha World-Herald*, December 23, 2003, 1B.

3. Sue Story Truax, "Eleanor Knoll Swanson Was Pioneering Lawyer," *Omaha World-Herald*, February 20, 2009, 5B.

4. Shugrue interview.

5. "Joins Law Firm," *Omaha World-Herald*, May 3, 1961, 45.

6. "Attorney Named Woman of the Year," *Omaha World-Herald*, May 4, 1976, 12.

7. Truax, "Eleanor Knoll Swanson," 6B.

8. Truax, "Eleanor Knoll Swanson," 6B.

9. Shugrue interview.

10. Friedman, *America's First Woman Lawyer*, 22.

11. Nebraska State Bar Association, *First 100 Women Lawyers in Nebraska*, 17–19.

12. Knoll, *Prairie University*, 50.

13. Mihelich, *History of Creighton University*, 104.

14. Knoll, *Prairie University*, 51.

15. Shugrue interview.

16. Shugrue interview.

17. "Elizabeth Davis Pittman, Nebraska's First Black Judge, Left an Admirable Legacy," Omaha.com, February 9, 2019.

18. "Elizabeth Davis Pittman."

19. "Elizabeth Davis Pittman."

20. Deborah Alexander, "Judge Colleen Buckley Believed in Tough Love," *Omaha World-Herald*, March 11, 1998, 4A.

21. Sue Story Truax, "Public Service Was Important to Ex-NU Regent Rosemary Skrupa," Omaha.com, October 26, 2013.

22. Truax, "Public Service."

23. Truax, "Public Service."

13. Government

1. Carol Ebdon, professor at University of Nebraska at Omaha and former Omaha finance director, interview by author, April 3, 2019.

2. Robert McMorris, "Betty Abbott: No Regrets, Only Future Plans," *Omaha World-Herald*, March 4, 1978, 17.

3. "Betty Abbott—No Disgrace Here," *Omaha World-Herald*, December 14, 2005, 6B; Mick Rood and Kathy Micek, "Clean Air, Urban Life Quality among Betty Abbott's Goals," *Omaha Sun Newspapers*, December 29, 1970.

4. Rood and Micek, "Clean Air, Urban Life."

5. James Denney, "Betty Abbott Isn't Far from Action," *Omaha World-Herald*, September 1, 1985.

6. McMorris, "Betty Abbott: No Regrets," 17.

7. "Betty Abbott—No Disgrace."

8. "Omaha Parks Board Bids Adieu to Gallagher," *Omaha-World-Herald*, October 13, 1968.

9. Elizabeth Flynn, "Articulate, Tireless Champion of Parks," *Omaha World-Herald*, September 13, 1970, 1E.

10. Kate Tukey Ross, "Mrs. Gallagher: Woman of Action," *Omaha World-Herald Magazine*, January 8, 1950.

11. Marge Hall Walsh, "It's 'Busy-ness' That Counts," in Gallagher, *Life and Times of the Gallagher Family*, 153.

12. Ross, "Mrs. Gallagher."

13. Rosemary Madison, "Rachel Gallagher Rarely Seen in Repose," *Omaha Sun*, August 20, 1964, 1.

14. Flynn, "Articulate, Tireless Champion," 1E.

15. "Rachel K. Gallagher Park Officially Named, Dedicated," *Omaha World-Herald*, August 3, 1955.

16. Gallagher, *Life and Times of the Gallagher Family*, 124.

17. Walsh, "It's 'Busy-ness,'" 153.

18. Gallagher, *Life and Times*, 150.

19. Gallagher, *Life and Times*, 151–56, 168.

20. Wirth, *Omaha's Henry Doorly Zoo*, 21.

21. Wirth, *Omaha's Henry Doorly Zoo*, 21.

22. Kay D. Clark letter to Larry Shoemaker, August 24, 1964, in Wirth, *Omaha's Henry Doorly Zoo*, 22.

23. Margaret Doorly letter, in Wirth, *Omaha's Henry Doorly Zoo*, 21.

24. Wirth, *Omaha's Henry Doorly Zoo*, 23.

25. C. David Kotok, "Friends Give Mary Cornett Fitting Send Off," *Omaha World-Herald*, August 2, 2007, 8B.

26. Buster Brown, retired Omaha city clerk, interview by author, April 4, 2019.

27. Mick Rood, "She Gets the Job Done," *Omaha Sun Newspapers*, June 15, 1972, 2.

28. Judith Nygren, "Longtime City Clerk Cornett Dies at 82," *Omaha World-Herald*, July 30, 2007, 4B.

29. Brown interview.

30. Nichole Aksamit, "Sprague Street May Honor Ruth Jackson," *Omaha World-Herald*, January 28, 2003, 3B.

31. Paul Landow, professor at University of Nebraska at Omaha and former mayor's chief of staff, interview by author, April 3, 2019.

32. Erin Grace, "Ex–Human Relations Director Ruth Jackson Dies at Age 75," *Omaha World-Herald*, October 28, 1998, 20.

33. Biga, "Carole Woods Harris."

34. Biga, "Carole Woods Harris."

35. Biga, "Carole Woods Harris."

36. Michaela Saunders, "Woods Harris Plans to Give Up Education Seat," *Omaha World-Herald*, January 11, 2008, 3B.

37. Deborah Alexander, "New County Boss Kelley: It's a Relief," *Omaha World-Herald*, July 23, 1998, 11SF.

38. Ebdon interview.

39. Landow interview.

40. Landow interview.

14. Civil Rights

1. Bloomfield, *Impertinences*, 58.

2. Bloomfield, *Impertinences*, 60.

3. Bloomfield, *Impertinences*, 64.

4. Kelly, *Women of Nebraska Hall of Fame*, 42.

5. Chatelain, *24th and Glory*, 104.

6. Chatelain, *24th and Glory*, 13.

7. Wirth, *From Society Page to Front Page*, 138–39.

8. Wirth, *From Society Page to Front Page*, 142.

9. Wirth, *From Society Page to Front Page*, 142.

10. Wirth, *From Society Page to Front Page*, 140.

11. Wirth, *From Society Page to Front Page*, 141–42.

12. Holland, *Ahead of Their Time*, 23.

13. Holland, *Ahead of Their Time*, 9–11.

14. Holland, *Ahead of Their Time*, 61.

15. Holland, *Ahead of Their Time*, 45.

16. Holland, *Ahead of Their Time*, 90–91.

17. Holland, *Ahead of Their Time*, 102.

18. Holland, *Ahead of Their Time*, 73.

19. Holland, *Ahead of Their Time*, 34.

20. "Bertha Calloway—Invaluable Connections," *Omaha World-Herald*, December 2, 2017, 6.

21. Holland, *Ahead of Their Time*, 91.

22. Virginia Walsh, former member of DePorres Club and social activist, interview by author, September 30, 2019.

23. Chatelain, *24th and Glory*, 104.

24. Rev. Darryl Eure, pastor and son of Dorothy Eure, interview by author, October 16, 2019.

25. Eure interview.

26. Eure interview.

27. Eure interview.

28. Eure interview.

29. Eure interview.

30. Chatelain, *24th and Glory*, 81–82.

31. Judith Nygren, "Activist Rowena Moore Dies; Fought Discriminatory Housing," *Omaha World-Herald*, January 1, 1999, 13; "Rowena Moore," Wikipedia, accessed September 24, 2019, https://en.wikipedia.org/wiki/Rowena_Moore.

32. Eure interview.

15. After the Women's Movement

1. Gail Walling Yanney, MD, physician and philanthropist, interview by author, January 29, 2020.

2. Michelle Zych, former executive director of the Women's Fund of Omaha, interview by author, February 11, 2020.

3. Yanney interview.

4. Zych interview.

5. Zych interview.

Bibliography

Published Works

"130 Years & Going Strong." *Alumni Times* (Summer 2018): 11–13.

Andrews-Koryta, Stepanka. "Dr. Olga Stastny, Her Service to Nebraska and the World." *Nebraska History* 68 (1987): 20–27.

Beveridge, Andrew, Susan Weber, and Sydney Beveridge. "Librarians in the U.S. from 1880–2009." *Oxford University Press Blog*, June 20, 2011. https://blog.oup.com/2011/06/librarian-census.

Biga, Leo. "Carole Woods Harris Makes a Habit of Breaking Barriers for Black Women in Business and Politics." *Leo Adam Biga's Blog*. Accessed April 24, 2019. http://leoadambiga.com./2012.

———. "Charles Hall's Fair Deal Café." *Leo Adam Biga's Blog*. Accessed September 16, 2019. http://leoadambiga.com/2016.

Bloomfield, Susanne George. *Impertinences*. Lincoln: University of Nebraska Press, 2005.

Blumenthal, Karen. *Let Me Play*. New York: Atheneum Books for Young Readers, 2005.

Boys Town. Directed by Norman Taurog. Omaha and Boys Town NE: MGM, 1938. Accessed via YouTube.

Bristow, David. *A Dirty Wicked Town: Tales of 19th Century Omaha*. Caldwell ID: Caxton Press, 2009.

———. "Mabel Gillespie One of the First Women Elected to Nebraska Legislature, Gretna, 1924." *Nebraska History Movement*, July 30, 2020.

———, ed. *Votes for Women: The 19th Amendment in Nebraska*. Lincoln: University of Nebraska Press, 2019.

Broadfield, William. *Stories of Omaha*. Omaha: Nichols and Broadfield, 1898.

Burbach, Karen. "Dr. Rena Boyle, Former Nursing Dean, Dies." University of Nebraska Medical Center, July 13, 2006. www.unmc.edu/news.

Burkley, Frank. *Faded Frontier*. Omaha: Burkley Envelope and Printing Co., 1935.

Callan, Louise. *The Society of the Sacred Heart in North America*. New York: Longmans Green & Co., 1937.

Carey, Fred. *Romance of Omaha*. Omaha: Bee-News, 1929.

Chatelain, Dirk. *24th and Glory*. Lincoln: History Nebraska, 2019.

Clark Potter, Fanny. "Historical Sketch of Brownell Hall, 1863–1864, 1913–14." NEGenWeb Project Resource Center, Online Library, Brownell Hall. Reproduced 2005. Accessed February 13, 2019. http://www.usgennet.org/usa/ne/topic/resources/OLLibrary /Brownell_Hall/index.htm.

Collins, Gail. *America's Women*. New York: HarperCollins, 2003.

Combs, Barry, and Jim Wigton. *Central High School Historical Timeline, 1854–2016*. December 21, 2016. Online PDF. https://www.chsfomaha.org/images/Documents /Historical-Timeline-Optimized.pdf.

Curley, Edwin A. *Nebraska 1875*. Lincoln: University of Nebraska Press, 2006.

Dawn of the Century, 1900–1910. Our American Century. Alexandria VA: Time-Life Books, 1998.

Derks, Scott. *Working Americans, 1880–2005*, vol. 4: *Women at Work*. Millerton NY: Grey House Publishing, 2005.

Diffendal, Anne P. "The LaFlesche Sisters: Susette, Rosalee, Margueritte, Lucy, Susan." In *Perspectives: Women in Nebraska History*, edited by Susan Pierce, 216–24. Lincoln: Nebraska Education Department and the Nebraska State Council for the Social Studies, 1984.

Duchesne: One Hundred Years of Growth in Love and Learning. Omaha: Duchesne Academy of the Sacred Heart, 1981.

Dunbier, Lonnie Pierson. *Their Place, Their Time: Women Artists in Nebraska, 1825–1945*. Museum of Nebraska Art Project. Omaha.

Dustin, Dorothy Devereux. *Omaha and Douglas County, a Panoramic History*. Woodland Hills CA: Windsor Publications, 1980.

Enns, Chris. "Wild Women Wednesday: Josie Washburn." *Cowgirl Magazine*, December 23, 2015. https://cowgirlmagazine.com/wild-women-wednesday-josie-washburn.

Federal Writers' Project. Works Progress Administration, Nebraska. *Omaha Guide to City and County*. Omaha: Omaha Public Library, 1935–39.

Fogarty, Joan. *Building Omaha*. Self-published, Omaha, 2013.

Friedman, Jane. *America's First Woman Lawyer*. Buffalo NY: Prometheus Books, 1993.

Gallagher, Jean Dudley. *The Life and Times of the Gallagher Family*. Self-published, 2002.

Gattey, Charles Neilson. *The Bloomer Girls*. New York: Coward-McCann, 1967.

Giffen, Fannie Reed, with illustrations by Bright Eyes LaFlesche. *Oo-Mah-Ha Ta-Wa-Tha (Omaha City)*. 1898. Reprint, Omaha: River Junction Press, 1998.

Goldblatt, David. *The Games*. New York: Norton, 2016.

Governor's Commission on the Status of Women. *Nebraska Women through the Years, 1867–1967*. Lincoln: Johnson Publishing Co., 1967.

Haynes, James. *History of the Trans-Mississippi and International Exposition of 1898*. St. Louis: Trans-Mississippi Exposition Board of Governors, 1910.

Hickman, Laura McKee. "Thou Shalt Not Vote: Anti-Suffrage in Nebraska, 1914–1920." *Nebraska History* 80 (1999): 55–65.

Hoctor, Emmett. "The Case of the Mysterious Magnanimous Madam." *Violent Kin* 37 (1998): 2–14.

Holland, Matt. *Ahead of Their Time*. Omaha: Self-published, 2014.

Junior League of Omaha. "Historical Summary of the Junior League of Omaha." *The Junior League of Omaha, Inc., Sixty-Fifth Annual Report*. Omaha: Junior League of Omaha, 1984.

———. *A Toast to Omaha*. N.p.: Quebecor Books, 2006.

Kalisch, Philip A. "The Early History of the Omaha Public Library." Master's thesis, Municipal University of Omaha, March 1964.

Katz, Wendy Jean. *The Trans-Mississippi and International Expositions of 1898–1899*. Lincoln: University of Nebraska Press, 2018.

Kelly, Peggy Volzke. *Women of Nebraska Hall of Fame*. Omaha: Nebraska International Women's Year Coalition, 1976.

Kiper, Daniel. *The Joslyns of Lynhurst*. Lincoln: Universe, 2006.

Klein, Maury. *Union Pacific*. Garden City NY: Doubleday, 1987.

Knoll, Robert. *Prairie University: A History of the University of Nebraska*. Lincoln: University of Nebraska Press, 1995.

Larsen, Lawrence, and Barbara Cottrell. *The Gate City*. Lincoln: University of Nebraska Press, 1982.

Lenhoff, Henry. *A History of Bishop Clarkson Memorial Hospital*. Omaha: University of Nebraska Medical Center, 1987.

Limprecht, Hollis. *The Kiewit Story*. Omaha: Omaha World-Herald Co., 1981.

Lindell, Lisa. "'The Nebraska Cyclone': Lillie Williams and the Embrace of Sport and Spectacle." *Nebraska History* 100, no. 4 (Winter 2019): 194–209.

Luebke, Frederick. *Nebraska: An Illustrated History*. Lincoln: University of Nebraska Press, 1995.

Lynch, Thomas, and Terry Hyland. *The Boys Town Story: 100 Years*. Virginia Beach VA: Downing Co. Publishers, 2016.

M., Shane, Eh Ree T., and Ty Asia B. "Fighting for Equality: Women Take a Stand." *Making Invisible Histories Visible*. Accessed September 24, 2019, https://invisiblehistory.ops.org.

Macy, Sue. *Wheels of Change*. Washington DC: National Geographic, 2011.

Menard, Orville D. *Political Bossism in Mid-America*. Lanham MD: University Press of America, 1989.

Mihelich, Dennis. *The History of Creighton University, 1878–2003*. Omaha: Creighton University Press, 2006.

Muldrey, Sister Mary Hermenia. *Abounding in Mercy*. New Orleans: Habersham, 1988.

Mullenbach, Cheryl. "Matilda Fletcher Defies Baggage-Smashers." *Iowa History*, November 19, 2016.

"Muriel R. Frank: MOMS First Woman President." *Physicians Bulletin* (January–February 2016): 24–25.

Nebraska Biographical Directory. St. Clair Shores MI: Somerset Publishers, 1999.

Nebraska State Bar Association. *The First 100 Women Lawyers in Nebraska*. Archival collection. History Nebraska, 2000.

Nebraska State Council for the Social Studies and Nebraska Department of Education. *Perspectives: Women in Nebraska History*. Edited by Susan Pierce. Lincoln: Nebraska Department of Education, Lincoln, 1984.

O'Brien, Kathleen. *Journeys*. Omaha: Sisters of Mercy, 1987.

Olson, James C. *History of Nebraska*. 2nd ed. Lincoln: University of Nebraska Press, 1966.

Oursler, Fulton, and Will Oursler. *Father Flanagan of Boys Town*. Garden City NY: Doubleday, 1959.

Paulman, Audrey, and John Schlelcher. "A History of Omaha's Unrivaled Facilities." *Physicians Bulletin* (January–February 2016): 14–15.

Polk, Donna Mays. *Black Men and Women of Nebraska*. Lincoln: Nebraska Black History Preservation Society, 1981.

Pollak, Oliver. *Welcome to Omaha*. Charleston SC: Arcadia Press, 2018.

Pollak, Oliver, and Les Valentine. *University of Nebraska at Omaha*. Charleston SC: Arcadia Publishing, 2007.

Potter, James. *Standing Firmly by the Flag*. Lincoln: University of Nebraska Press, 2012.

Pratt, William. "'Union Maids' in Omaha Labor History, 1887–1945." In *Perspectives: Women in Nebraska History*, edited by Susan Pierce, 196–202. Lincoln: Nebraska Department of Education and the Nebraska State Council for the Social Studies, 1984.

Prelude to the Century, 1870–1900. Edited by Time-Life Books. Alexandria VA: Time-Life Books, 1999.

Quest, Tom. *Duchesne College & Academy*. Omaha: Duchesne Academy of the Sacred Heart, 2017.

Rea, Liz. *Omaha / Douglas County History Timeline History at a Glance*. Douglas County Historical Society, 2004, reprinted 2007. Online PDF. http://www.douglascohistory .net/History%20at%20a%20Glance%209-2007.pdf.

Reese, William J. *The Origins of the American High School*. New Haven CT: Yale University Press, 1995.

Regan, Sister M. Joanna. *Tender Courage*. Gwynedd Valley PA: Gwynedd-Mercy College, 1978.

Reilly, Hugh, and Kevin Warneke. *Father Flanagan of Boys Town*. Boys Town NE: Boys Town Press, 2008.

Reiner, Kim. *Lost Restaurants of Omaha*. Charleston SC: History Press, 2017.

Rippey, James. *Goodbye Central: Hello World*. Davenport IA: Wagner Printers, 1975.

Sasse, Adam. "A History of North Omaha's Immanuel Hospital." *North Omaha History*, August 28, 2015. https://northomahahistory.com/2015/08/28/a-history-of-immanuel -hospital-in-north-omaha.

Sorenson, Alfred. *The Story of Omaha*. 3rd ed. Omaha: National Printing Co., 1923.

Starita, Joe. *A Warrior of the People*. New York: St. Martin's Press, 2016.

Sullivan, Dan, ed. *The Nebraska 100*. Omaha: Omaha World-Herald, 2015.

Thompson, Tommy R. *A History of the University of Nebraska at Omaha, 1908–1983.* Dallas: Taylor Publishing Co., 1983.

Tyler, Albert, ed., and Ella Auerbach, comp. *History of Medicine in Nebraska.* Omaha: Magic City Printing Co., 1928.

Ware, Susan. *American Women's History.* Oxford: Oxford University Press, 2015.

Weiss, Elaine. *The Woman's Hour.* New York: Viking Press, 2018.

Wheeler, Wayne. *Almanac of Nebraska.* Baltimore: Park Bromwell Press, 1975.

Wilhite, Ann L. Wiegman. "Sixty-Five Years till Victory: A History of Woman Suffrage in Nebraska." *Nebraska History* 49 (1968): 149–63.

Windsor, Suzannah. "To See if Great Minds Really Do Think Alike: A Conversation between Grace Bauer and Laura Madeline Wiseman." *Compose Journal*, February 25, 2014. http://www.Composejournal.com/see.

Wirth, Eileen. *From Society Page to Front Page.* Lincoln: University of Nebraska Press, 2013.

———. "Heckling President Wilson: Omaha Suffragist Rheta Childe Dorr." In *Perspectives: Women in Nebraska History*, edited by Susan Pierce, 50–53. Lincoln: Nebraska Department of Education and the Nebraska State Council for the Social Studies, 1984.

———. *Omaha's Henry Doorly Zoo & Aquarium.* Charleston SC: History Press, 2017.

Wirth, Eileen, and Carol McCabe. *Omaha's Historic Houses of Worship.* Charleston SC: Arcadia Press, 2014.

Wiseman, Laura Madeline. "Grandma and Susan B. Anthony." *BroadBlogs*, March 21, 2014. https://broadblogs.com/2014/03/21/grandma-and-susan-b-anthony.

———. "Researching and Writing about Ancestors." *Country Dog Review.* Accessed April 30, 2018, http://www.countrydogreview.org/Laura_Madeline_Wiseman.html.

Interviews

Allen, Elaine. Administrator, Mutual of Omaha. September 24, 2019.

Andersen, Marian. Omaha philanthropist and civic leader. April 15, 2019.

Ashford, Brad. Former Nebraska congressman and state senator. June 11, 2019.

Bieker, Margo. Volunteer archivist, Duchesne Academy. July 8, 2018.

Bigsby, Keith. Retired principal, Central High School. May 16, 2018.

Braden, Barbara. Retired dean and nursing professor, Creighton University. February 28, 2019.

Brown, Buster. Retired Omaha city clerk. April 4, 2019.

Claussen, Connie. Former head of women's athletics, University of Nebraska at Omaha. July 15, 2019.

Ebdon, Carol. Professor, University of Nebraska at Omaha, and former Omaha finance director. April 3, 2019.

Eure, Rev. Darryl. Pastor and son of Dorothy Eure. October 16, 2019.

Fogarty, Joan. Omaha historian and former staffer, Benson High School. January 21, 2019.

Gifford, Charles. Omaha architect and son of Emmy Gifford. February 8, 2019.

Grenzeback, Martha. Local history librarian, Omaha Public Library. January 10, 2018.

Haggart, Barbara. Retired executive, Greater Omaha Chamber of Commerce. May 20, 2019.

Higgins, Mary. President, Marian High School, and former women's coach, Creighton University. July 23, 2019.

Johnson, Carolyn. Descendant of Bright Eyes LaFlesche. April 18, 2019.

Johnson, Marguerite. Descendant of Bright Eyes LaFlesche. April 18, 2019.

Kauders, Audrey. Retired executive, Joslyn Art Museum. February 9, 2019.

Kawa, Jack. Retired owner of Johnny's Café. September 18, 2019.

Krecek, John. Retired Creighton University registrar, June 10, 2020.

Landow, Paul. Professor, University of Nebraska at Omaha, and former mayor's chief of staff. April 3, 2019.

Lynch, Thomas. Director, Boys Town Museum. May 2, 2019.

Maxwell, Mary. Creighton family descendant and public speaker. November 28, 2018.

McGill, Ann. Creighton family descendant. December 11, 2018.

Mclarney, Michael. Former director, United Way of the Midlands. April 23, 2019.

Mihelich, Dennis. Retired professor of history, Creighton University. November 27, 2018.

Mitchell, Rudi. Former chairman of the Omaha Tribe, June 18, 2020.

Monson, Mary. Retired history teacher, Duchesne Academy. December 19, 2018.

O'Brien, Kathleen, RSM. Late historian, the Sisters of Mercy. January 9, 2018.

Paulman, Audrey. Physician, University of Nebraska Medical Center. February 22, 2019.

Peters, David. Head of school, Mount Michael Benedictine School. January 21, 2019.

Rader, Benjamin. Retired professor of history, University of Nebraska–Lincoln. July 11, 2019.

Salerno, Jeanne. Former president, the Junior League of Omaha. February 5, 2019.

Severin, Susan, RSM. Archivist, Sisters of Mercy. January 8, 2019.

Shugrue, Richard. Retired professor of law, Creighton University. February 18, 2019.

Shukert, Martin. Principal, RDG Shukert, and former Omaha planning director. June 14, 2019.

Smith, Penelope. Former archivist, Joslyn Castle. December 17, 2018.

Spellman, Connie. Retired director of Omaha by Design. December 20, 2019.

Steinberg, James. Physician and son of Dr. Muriel Frank. February 23, 2019.

Stoney, Janice. Retired CEO, Northwestern Bell Telephone Co. June 8, 2019.

Sullivan, Lynn. Local historian, Omaha Public Library. June 25, 2018.

Thomas, Jann and Lawrence. Outstanding golfer and civic leaders. August 1, 2019.

Trebbien, Jim. Retired dean, Metropolitan Community College Culinary Arts Program. August 12, 2019.

Velder, Debra. Retired executive, Nebraska School Activities Association. August 1, 2019.

Walsh, Virginia. Former member of DePorres Club and social activist. September 30, 2019.

Wilson, Scott. History teacher, Central High School. November 11, 2019.

Wiseman, Laura Madeline. Expert on suffragist Madeline Fletcher. April 30, 2018.

Yanney, Gail Walling, MD. Physician and philanthropist. January 29, 2020.

Ziegenbein, Lyn Wallin. Retired executive director, Peter Kiewit Foundation. June 4, 2019.

Zych, Michelle. Former executive director of the Women's Fund of Omaha. February 11, 2020.

Index

journalists, xiii. *See also specific journalists*
Junior League of Omaha (JLO), 78–79, 80, 82,
    92, 146, 166

KANEKO, 95, 96
Kaneko, Jun, 95, 96
Kaneko, Ree Schonlau, 95–96
Kansas City Call, 10
Kauders, Audrey, 17, 93, 94, 95, 96
Kawa family, 118
Keen, Octa, 35
Kelley, Kathleen, 152
Kennison, Patrick, 129
Kiddie Kollege, 81
Kiewit, Anna, 104
Kiewit, Peter, 104
Kimball, Mrs. Thomas L., 55, 73
King Science Center, 162
Kirksey, Ellisa, 10
Kleine, Don, 140, 141
Knolla, Michelle, 69
Kozlik, Emily Cunningham, 79
Krecek, John, 32–33
Krug Amusement Center, 146–47

Labedz, Bernice, 143, 151
Ladies' Temperance Society, 42
LaFlesche, Joseph, 27, 28–29, 30
LaFlesche, Susan, 32, 34
LaFlesche, Susette "Bright Eyes": about, 27,
    28, 29, 34; advocacy of, 31–32; Standing Bear
    and, 30–31; Trans-Mississippi Exposition
    and, 32–33
Lakota Tribe, 32, 35
Landow, Paul, 152, 153
law, 137–42
lawyers, women. *See* attorneys, women
lay women in Catholic schools, 15–16
Leadership Omaha, 113
League of Women Voters, 69, 144
Leahy, Don, 128
Lee, Mabel, 125–26
Legal Aid Society, 161
Libor, Josef and Ann, 117–18
libraries, public, 87, 90
Lily, 42–43
Lincoln law college, 139

Lindsey, Kelly, 131
Lininger, George W., 87
Little Italy, 74, 100–101, 115–16
Logan, Cheryl, 12–13, 163
Lutherans, 45, 60
Lynch, Thomas, 76, 77
Lynhurst, 89

MacMurphy, Harriet Dakin, 17, 39
Magee, Nellie, 72
Malcolm X, 155, 162–63
Marcuzzo, Guiseppina, 115–16
Margaret Fuller Society, 8
Marian High School, 15, 16, 127–28, 131
Markoe, John, 158–59
Markoe, William, 158
Martin, E. F., 52, 53, 56–57
Mary Cooper Dance Studio, 91
Maxwell, Mary, 20
Mayor's Commission on the Status of Women,
    134, 168
McDonald, Alan, 90, 91
McDonald, John, 90
McGill, Ann, 19
McHugh, Kate, 9–10
McKinley, William, 33, 88
Mclarney, Michael, 72, 79–80, 83
McMorris, Robert, 55
McNamara, Mary, 10–11
medallion competition, 85–86
Medical Visitor, 66
Mellen, Ann, 120
Mercy High School, 15
Metropolitan Entertainment & Convention
    Authority (MECA), 153
Metropolitan Omaha Medical Society, 68, 69
Mihelich, Dennis, 19
Mildred Brown Strolling Park, 158
Missouri tribe, 2
Mitchell, Rudi, 35
Monson, Mary, 23, 24
Moore, Rowena, 162–63
Moot Court competition, 137–38
Mothers for Self Help, 81
Mothers Guild, 77
Mount Saint Mary's Academy, 14–15

Printed in the USA
CPSIA information can be obtained
at www.ICGtesting.com
CBHW021444190224
4471CB00002B/68